THE TIME OF MY LIVES

Maureen,
Just the way
you are

Tell Ome

THE TIME OF MY LIVES

*Lived and Written by
J.M. Valente*

Cover Design by J.M. Valente

Copyright © 2009 by J.M. Valente.

Library of Congress Control Number: 2009910056
ISBN: Hardcover   978-1-4415-8139-6
              Softcover   978-1-4415-8138-9

All rights reserved. No part of this book may be reproduced or transmitted in any form or by any means, electronic or mechanical, including photocopying, recording, or by any information storage and retrieval system, without permission in writing from the copyright owner.

This book was printed in the United States of America.

To order additional copies of this book, contact:
Xlibris Corporation
1-888-795-4274
www.Xlibris.com
Orders@Xlibris.com
67315

Contents

Chapter One-Part One	Life Accelerated	11
Chapter One-Part Two	Patricia	14
Chapter Two-Part One	Mary/Joey	20
Chapter Two-Part Two	Mary, Me, and ?	25
Chapter Three-Part One	New People, Places, and Things	29
Chapter Three-Part Two	Big City Nights, Big City Lights	36
Chapter Four-Part One	The Rude Awakening	41
Chapter Four-Part Two	New Place, Little Space	52
Chapter Five-Part One	The Revolving Door of Life	57
Chapter Five-Part Two	An Unforgivable Invasion	64
Chapter Six-Part One	Running Around Again	71
Chapter Six-Part Two	The Truth at Last	78
Chapter Seven-Part One	When It Rains, It Pours!	86
Chapter Seven-Part Two	More Heavy Weather!	94
Chapter Eight-Part One	Stark Realities	100
Chapter Eight-Part Two	All Things Have an Ending	107
Chapter Nine-Part One	By Its Cover	114
Chapter Nine-Part Two	The Undiscovered Country	127
Chapter Ten-Part One	Love's Labors Lost	140
Chapter Ten-Part Two	Reunions/Deceleration	157

Dedicated to
The Ten

Foreword

Jim is a man who is irreproachable. What is outside and what's inside are conflicting. I see warmth that is buried by hurt and disappointment. There is a lasting bitterness he carries. He is capable of giving in a relationship, but his lack of trust keeps him from doing so.

An excerpt from the diary
of a female friend (circa 1980)

Chapter One-Part One

Life Accelerated

1952 Autumn

I WAS BORN the third child of Ellie and Joseph in the fall of 1952, just after midnight of September the twenty-third, having a brother, Joseph Jr. (1948), and a sister, Debra (1950), before me.

Life for me didn't get off to a very good start. I was stricken with polio at about three years old. Completely paralyzed, I could only move my eyes, had to be taught to answer yes or no by blinking my eyes. I would spend the next year and a half living in the capital city's major hospital. After about a year of treatment, which got me movement back to my waist, my legs weren't showing any results; so the doctors then condemned me to a wheelchair for the rest of my life.

One of my therapy nurses, whose name is lost to me, asked my mother for more time with me. My mother, feeling there was nothing to lose, agreed.

The nurse would tell me every day that if I could move the pedals of the stationary tricycle, it would take me home.

Well, I guess you could say a miracle happened because at the end of my one and a half years stay in the hospital, I made it home.

Had to learn how to walk all over again with the help of leg braces for a while worn on the outside of my pants like the ones *Forrest Gump* wore in his movie. It was tough being four and dealing with that. I do remember being made fun of a lot; children can be very cruel.

I guess I felt—no, I know I felt—left behind, in so many aspects, such as learning to do things like riding a bicycle later than the other children in my neighborhood.

Not wanting to be left behind ever again, I subconsciously accelerated my life, not knowing at the time this wasn't a really good thing to do.

Hindsight is twenty-twenty.

For example, in kindergarten at five years old, I got caught by the teacher kissing / *makin' out* with a girl, Susan, in the coat closet. I was sent to the office where my mother was called to come and pick me up. She told me kissing girls is okay but not in school.

I graduated from kindergarten with that girl by my side, my graduation partner. I guess she liked the way I kissed.

Wow! A good kisser at five!

1958

At the age of six, an unplanned child was born into my family, another sister, Valerie. This kind of threw things off balance. My parents had planned on three children. She became the center of attention, which took it away from me. Joey, Deb, and I had to share things such as a record player, radio, etc., whereas Valerie got her own.

In spite of that, my childhood was okay. My father provided needed things—house, food, clothing, etc.—while my mother supplied the love, affection, understanding, attention, and anything else my father didn't or couldn't. His way of keeping order was physical punishment for his sons. But not for his daughters; Mom would take care of them.

We more feared him than loved and/or respected him.

I never was very close to my father until my mother died. You see, my brother was my father's son, while I was my mother's son. That was okay with me; I loved her more anyway.

That made it my brother's duty to follow in our father's footsteps, in the field of masonry construction, which I didn't want to.

Speaking of my brother, Joey, I loved him very much; as a matter of fact, I idolized him. He was very handsome; he had blue eyes, black hair, just like Elvis "the King" Presley.

All the girls wanted to be with him, all the guys wanted to be him, the overflow of girls came to me, "Joey's little brother." This and being the singer in my little local rock-and-roll band called the Optic Illusion accelerated my sex life, for instance.

1965 Summer

I lost my virginity at thirteen to eighteen-year-old Wendy who really wanted my brother but settled for me. I had no problem with that, for she had the looks and the body to go with it. The best thing that came out of this encounter was not just me.

She taught me not to rush sex, take my time, be gentle, and listen to her instructions.

It was quite the seduction scene.

I don't think I should go into the details.

At about this time, unknown to me, my brother, Joey, was starting to use illegal drugs.

I will relate to that a little later.

Chapter One-Part Two

Patricia

1965 Autumn

PATRICIA MOVED TO my city, I have forgotten from where. I will never forget her being introduced in my eighth-grade homeroom. I was incredibly taken by her. To me, she was the prettiest girl I had ever seen. She had blond hair never shorter than shoulder-length, blue eyes, full lips, average figure for her age—not outstanding, but there was enough of everything. Think of Tuesday Weld / Thalia from the *Dobie Gillis* television show or Judy Geeson / Pamela in the movie *To Sir with Love*. Patricia was one of those girls that were so good-looking that all the other girls didn't like her. I had to be with her, and I would as soon as I got rid of the girl I was seeing, who was just a big tease.

We played at being lovers, but nothing really happened; she would only go so far. I was ready to go all the way. My chance would come as soon as the next dance came up. Patricia was there, and I wasted no time in my pursuit for her affections.

Dancing slow with her, holding her close to me, whispering sweet things in her ear, I won her over.

Yes, she came to be my first real steady girlfriend and lover. We were both fourteen years old, and what we felt was love.

1965 Winter

(◊ "Gimme Some Lovin'"◊ The Spencer Davis Group, 1967)

I remember our first sexual encounter. After school, I would go to Patty's house to do "homework" (ha-ha). Her mother was divorced, so she worked every day until five o'clock. On this particular day, when I got to her house, Patricia was starting to feel sick. She felt she needed to take some cold medicine and get into bed. She changed into what I felt was a very sexy little blue sheer nylon baby-doll nightie.

This got me very excited, especially when she wanted me to get into the bed with her. At first, I said, "I really should go home."

She started to cry and told me she wanted me to stay. How could I refuse? I undressed to my briefs, got into her bed; we began to watch the movie *Lonely Are the Brave* on television. Well, I could not keep my hands off her. One thing led to another, and before long, we were having sex. It was her first time, which made it a little difficult to make penetration. It was my first time with someone I had real feelings for, so I guess you could say it was a first for both of us.

After that day, she would wear one of my T-shirts that she had written "**JIM'S**" on, meaning she was my girl. We made love every chance we got.

(◊ "Good Day, Sunshine"◊ Beatles, 1965)

Saturday-Night Babysitting

Patricia had a younger half brother, Richey. She and I would babysit him on Saturday nights when her mother went out with her boyfriend. Let me relate the Saturday-night babysitting.

I would hang out with the guys on the corner up the end of Patty's street until about eight at night.

One of those many nights, one of the guys proclaimed to me,

"We all talk and lie about getting sex, and you never say anything, but we all know you're the only one that's really getting it."

No comment from me. I had learned to be discreet very early in life. The less said the better!

Like I was saying, I was hanging out, waiting for Patty's mother to leave. Didn't want her there when I arrived; neither did Patty.

We would start the evening sitting on the couch, watching television. After she got her brother to go to bed, Patty would then get comfortable by changing into one of her sheer nylon baby-doll nighties, which she had now come to know was something that really turned me on. We would start with foreplay on the couch and then eventually make our way to her bedroom.

At fourteen, I was having Saturday nights that most men twice my age desired and only dreamt about.

After we were finished with the lovemaking a.k.a. intercourse, Patty would make me something to eat. All that activity would make a young man very hungry. I stayed a little while after that and then left to make it home by eleven.

I have to say, it was a good time in my life because I remember it like it was yesterday. Our relationship went on until the end of ninth grade. Now we were both fifteen years old; and for some reason, lost to my memory, we split up. Patty started seeing Louie, who had just split from his girlfriend, Mary, my future wife. Patty didn't want to have sex with anyone else right away; in the sixties, that was being a whore. So I offered her my services and told her she could use me for what we now know as booty calls.

(◊ "You Don't Have to Say You Love Me"◊ Dusty Springfield, 1966)

1966 Summer

The Funny Louie Story

One afternoon, Patty and I had just finished up a booty call.

We were surprised by Louie, her new boyfriend, coming to Patty's house unexpectedly.

Neither of us wanted him to see us together as I was now seeing Louie's ex-girlfriend, Mary (you could say Louie and I traded up). Patty really didn't want to let him in. I told her to talk to him through the door while I went out the back way. I cut through the backyards and came around the block to see him sitting on her front steps looking rather gloomy.

"Hey, Louie. What's wrong, man?" I asked him.

"Hi, Jim. Patty won't open the door and let me in. I think she's got someone in the house, another guy," he answered.

"I know her, she wouldn't do that to you. Come on, Louie, let me see if I can get her to open the door," I said, trying to be helpful.

She finally did open the door for us, which was right as I asked her to.

Before she could say a word, I very quickly said to her, "You don't look very good, are you feeling sick?" *Wink! Wink!*

"Yes, I was in bed, sick, when Louie started knocking on the door. I got up to see who it was. I wasn't looking very good, so I really didn't want to be seen like that. When he stopped knocking, I went to the bathroom to clean up a bit. That's when I heard your voice asking me to open the door because Louie thinks I have someone in here. That made me decide to open the door and show him that no one was home but me," she answered.

I then turned to Louie and said, "Come on, man. Let's take a look around and see if she has anyone in here!"

There was no one to be found, of course.

I advised him, "Hey, man, stop overreacting and start trusting her," and then went on my way.

To this day, I believe Louie never found out what really took place that day.

1966 Winter

The Ben Hur Freezer Incident!

To begin with, my parents had a very large Ben Hur lift-top freezer in the finished basement of our house, where we would have house parties. One winter night, right after returning home from Mary's house, I would always go into the basement and call Mary to let her know I got home safely. I hung up the phone with her, and suddenly, it rang. I quickly picked it up so as not to wake anybody in the house.

To my pleasant surprise, it was Patty, wanting to be with me—you know, the booty call thing. You see, I had not gotten intimate with Mary yet, so this was working out great for me.

I told her, "I can't leave the house, I just got home. Can't this wait until tomorrow afternoon?"

"No, it can't! I'll come there," she insisted.

"Okay, come to the back door, knock softly. I will be waiting just inside the door," I instructed her.

She walked, slightly more than a mile to my house.

Keep in mind, neither one of us had a driver's license or car, and it was very cold outside.

I sat waiting on a staircase that led down from the kitchen to an area we called the washroom—you know, where there was a sink, half bath, washing machine, and dryer. And also some shelves where canned food were kept.

This room had three doors. The one to my left would be the one where Patty would be knocking.

The one to my right led into the garage.

The third door was at the top of the staircase where I sat at the bottom. These doors were normally kept closed. So we would be somewhat isolated from the rest of the house. To my immediate right, there was a short stairway leading down the opposite direction into the finished basement *where the freezer was.*

(◊ "The Look of Love"◊ Dusty Springfield, 1966)

After about twenty minutes, there came a soft knock on the door.

I opened the door with mixed feelings. She, however, knew exactly how she felt—very horny. We went into the basement, talked quietly, and tried to decide where to have this intimate encounter a.k.a. booty call. There was a big easy chair, but not big enough.

At about the same time, we both looked at the freezer. Realizing it was big enough to lie down on, we agreed it would be better than the floor.

She stayed for a little while after the somewhat uncomfortable encounter. We held each other in that aforementioned big chair.

I softly said, "It's very late. I do need to get some sleep. After all, it was a school night."

Sadly, she had to leave.

I told her, "I will be waiting for your phone call to let me know you made it home safely."

We kissed for what I didn't know then would be our last time.

Her phone call came about twenty minutes after she left; she had made it home safely. I answered it quickly so as not to let it have a full ring. "Hello, Patty?"

"Yes, Jim, thank you for tonight. I will always love you. Good night," she told me.

"Ya okay. Good night," I quietly and somewhat impassively replied.

I hung up the phone and shook my head, wondering if what had just happened really did or if I was really upstairs in my bed, asleep, dreaming this. Because of some physical evidence, I realized I was not dreaming and then went upstairs to bed.

This was the last time I would ever see or talk to Patricia. Sadly, to this day, I haven't had any contact with her. So I don't know how her life turned out. I do hope she got what she wanted in her life. Not knowing makes my heart feel as cold as the inside of that big ol' freezer.

End of Chapter One

Chapter Two-Part One

Mary/Joey

1966-67

AT THE BEGINNING of the winter of 1966, I started getting to know Mary, but it was not until early 1967 that our relationship really started to build momentum. I would hang out with her when I wasn't practicing with my band, the Optic Illusion, or trying to get a gig lined up. The band played at some parties. We never did get a chance to perform at any of the local dances, but we did do an after-school concert. The attendance was a full auditorium. Robert, the bass guitar player, and I had written an original song titled "I'm Gonna Miss Her," a slow ballad that the girls seemed to like hearing me sing.

Mary wasn't too happy about me getting a lot of attention from other girls. So the band didn't stay together too much longer. Mary wanted me to spend more time with her. So I lost the band and gained a lover.

A New Lover

(◊ "How Can I Be Sure?"◊ The Young Rascals, 1967)

It was the babysitting thing again. Mary would babysit her sister's three children on Saturday nights; she started wanting me to be there. Like with Patty, I would hang out with the guys for a while and then go to be with her. Mary was five feet two inches, a small blonde package of dynamite that looked very much like Barbara *Streisand* in the movie *The Owl and the Pussycat*. She always played it tough; it was just an act. Getting intimate with her, I saw her tender, loving, sexy side that she didn't show in public.

Our intimate interludes were at her sister's house after she got the kids to bed. We would then go into the dayroom at the front of her sister's house and use the daybed.

But it was at her house one afternoon, when her mother was at work, that we first made love; and yes, it was her first time.

I know what you're thinking: sounds familiar.

(◊ "La-La Means I Love You"◊ The Delfonics, 1968)

By this time, my brother, Joey, was using any and all the illegal drugs he could get his hands on. He wasn't looking good at all. The drugs were slowly taking his good looks and health, not to mention killing him. My father denied there was a problem with Joey's drug abuse. To him, only weak people used drugs in that way, and how could any son of his be that weak? He was very much a pompous ass, to put it lightly. My mother recognized the problem and begged my father to get Joey some professional medical help. They spent a lot of money getting him help, but it only worked for a while.

You see, my brother was a heroin user. A heavy heroin user.

(◊ "A Whiter Shade of Pale"◊ Procol Harum, 1967)

Joey wasn't too crazy about me seeing Mary and told her to stay away from me. It was far too late for that and for his drug problem.

He got worse; all he cared about now was getting money to buy heroin fixes or codeine to use between fixes.

I did what after-school work I could find. Joey knew this. So when he would see me, he'd ask me for money. Not knowing I was doing more harm than good, I would give it to him. After all, he was my brother, and I loved him very much. I'd do almost anything for him. Almost anything.

I have to pause here to say this is very hard for me to write about Joey; to write this, I have to relive it in my mind.

Things were only going to get worse. Winter was setting in, and my father had disowned my brother and would not allow him at the house.

Plus, the woman Joey married two years earlier, because she was knocked up, had thrown him out also.

They had a daughter, Sherry, my niece and godchild.

1968

Time marches on; it waits for no one. Joey's drug abuse was only getting worse. He looked like a monster: green eyes, yellow skin, and with no regular place to live. His hygiene suffered. Yeah, he smelled pretty bad. I don't believe he cared about it at this point.

He managed somehow to survive the spring and get to summer.

I, in the meantime, had finished my first year of high school, tenth grade, at my city's vocational high school, studying sheet metal.

Back then, high school was tenth, eleventh, and twelfth grades. I was looking forward to getting my first car.

My father helped me to get a summer job with one of his business associates. A heating and air-conditioning company that used sheet metal for ductwork. I really needed a car to get back and forth to work.

My sister, Debby, who was looking to getting a new car, sold to me her first car, a 1964 Ford Falcon.

I felt I was doing real well. I had a job, a car, and a girlfriend.

The only downside to my life now was my brother wasn't getting any better, and I didn't know what I could do to really help him.

One of the last times I saw him was in the late summer of 1968.

"You won't have to worry about me for much longer," he told to me.

I hopefully took this as him, meaning he was going to get better—you know, kick his drug habit and get back to having a regular life. I had always imagined us going through life together as brothers, friends, and business partners. Sorry to say, this was not meant to be.

For you see, in August, one unforgettable night, while sitting with Mary at her kitchen table, she got a phone call. She answered it, "Hello?" and then just listened to what the caller was saying.

She replied to the caller, saying, "Okay, thanks, he's here. I'll tell him."

She slowly hung up the phone, sat down facing me, took my hand, and looked into my eyes.

She tenderly started to relay the caller's message.

"That was a friend of mine calling to tell me they had just heard that something horrible has happened."

She stopped, looked down at the floor, and was no longer looking into my eyes. My stomach tightened. By reading her body language, I knew this was not going to be good news. Squeezing my hand tighter, she continued, "There's been a car accident. It's believed your brother, Joey, was killed!"

I stood up quickly and sharply replied, "No way, that can't be true. I just saw him. He didn't look too good, but he was alive!"

For you see, this was not something I wanted to believe. That my *only* brother was dead at twenty years old! After I collected my thoughts, I asked Mary, "Who was that on the phone? Someone who doesn't like me, playing some very cruel joke!"

As funny as it sounded, that's what I wanted to believe.

She replied, "Jim, please, this is not some kind of joke! You need to go home and find out what has really happened."

Go home—that's something I really didn't want to do right now; for at home would be the truth, and there was no way I wanted this to be true. There was a glimmer of hope in my heart that it wasn't true. My thoughts were racing. Maybe it was someone who borrowed his car.

I drove home quite slowly. I think you know why.

On the ride home, I told myself, *I don't want to believe this has happened. And would not, even if it were true*. I felt strongly that if I didn't believe it happened, then it didn't happen.

Was I making any sense?
Who was I kidding?
Answer: only myself.

Well, when I got to the house, there were several cars parked in front. Not a good sign. I went in the house; there were a lot of people there. I was standing just inside the front door, in the hallway that led to the kitchen. To my left was an archway into the living room with another archway at the far end into the dining room, where everyone was sitting. I overheard my father mutter the phrase "still wet behind the ears." That means that someone is very young or, in this case, was.

My mother approached me and started to say something. *I put my hand up as if to say stop*, and she went silent.

I proclaimed, "Mom, please, I'm really tired and need some sleep," and quickly made my way up the stairs, to my right, and into my bedroom. I sat on my bed, saying and thinking to myself,

This isn't happening. It's some kind of bad dream.

After a while, there was a gentle knock on my door.

"Yes, who is it?" I inquired.

It was my mother. *She poked her head through the doorway* and softly said,

"I guess you already know what has happened. The wake starts tomorrow."

"Know what! What wake! Please, I'm tired. Need to get some sleep. I have work tomorrow. Good night!" I replied harshly.

I lay there thinking about how badly I felt, talking to my mother that way. I closed my eyes and fell asleep.

I awoke early. No one else was up. Quietly I got dressed and left for work, hoping to avoid the first afternoon session of the wake, thinking, *What you don't see, you don't have to believe.*

I worked in the sheet metal shop that day, not out on an install.

At lunchtime, my boss came out of his office, approached me, put his hand on my shoulder, and asked, "Jim, are you okay?"

I replied, "Ya, why shouldn't I be?"

He answered, "Well, your mother just called to see if you here. She told me what has happened to your brother, and she really needs you at home. So as your boss, I'm ordering you to take the rest of the day off and come back to work when you feel up to it. As your friend, I'm telling you your mother needs you to be there for her and the family."

He was right, and to this day, his words still ring in my ears.

Reluctantly, I left to finally face the truth; the sad truth, the heartbreaking truth that I had lost my only brother and trusted friend.

Reluctantly, I attended the first evening session of the wake. It was very crowded. To face this terrible truth was one of the hardest things I've had to do in my life thus far. One I still have trouble with to this day.

Well, this part is easier said than it was done. I requested—no, I demanded—that on the day of the funeral, I would carry the front of Joey's casket to escort him to his final resting place. Doing that made me feel that I was helping him one last time. This would give me some consolation and closure.

(◊ "Daniel"◊ Elton John)

Chapter Two-Part Two

Mary, Me, and ?

(◊ *"Ob La Di, Ob La Da"*◊ *The Beatles*)

1969

LIFE DOES GO on, even when you think it shouldn't because you have lost something that you must now live without.

Mary and I seemed to have a good relationship going; we spent as much time as we could together. Oh sure, we had our rough patches, but we always seemed to work it out and stay together. We were young and full of love and energy. We would talk about the future and what we would like to see happen. I do believe, most of time, we felt we were truly in love with each other. I was looking forward to finishing high school and starting working full-time.

Okay, s—t happens! Yeah, happens when you actually don't want it to, so here's another example of my accelerated life.

Apparently, Mary and I were not being cautious enough with our lovemaking and had an oops. A very big oops. Because one fateful day, Mary told me she had missed her monthly visitor and was feeling sick in the mornings.

Yeah, you guessed it, she was knocked up!

We talked about what we should do and what we'd like to do. They became the same thing, and that was get married, have the baby, and raise it together the best we could. That wasn't really the hard part. You see, I was only seventeen. Mary was eighteen. I had to get my parents' permission and a judge's too. I acquired both. We were set; now the rest of the stuff:

marriage license, blood tests, and an appointment with the local justice of the peace.

Mary, who was now three months along, and I were married on January 29 of 1970, a Thursday evening, at the office of the local justice of the peace. After the ceremony, we went to dinner.

I, still attending high school, had to go in the following morning. We never actually had a honeymoon.

Mary had left high school before she started to show. I had to get my diploma so I could work and support a family. I graduated from the vocational high school a married man with a child on the way. Went to work full-time for the heating and air-conditioning company I had been with during the summers while still in school. My mom, God bless her, convinced my dad into buying a multifamily house where Mary, me, and ? would live on the first floor.

While waiting for this to happen, I would stay at my parents' house during the week, Mary at her mother's. I would join Mary at her mom's house on the weekends.

This went on until the end of May. In early June, we moved into the five-room first-floor apartment of the multifamily house my parents had bought.

On the sixteenth of July 1970, our first son, Jim II, was born; we were now a family. At seventeen, I was a husband and a father. The first four years of our marriage seemed to go satisfactorily. Some problems, but nothing we couldn't deal with or work out. In the third year of our union, we were blessed with a second son, Vincent, coming along in 1973 on the twenty-eighth of July.

1973 Late Winter

Bad news! Mary was pregnant again, and we were struggling to make ends meet with the two children we had. We definitely didn't have room, physically and/or financially, for another child.

Also, I had just been laid off for the second time; my income was in jeopardy. Unemployment checks were not a lot of money. We knew we could not afford to have another child.

A choice had to be made: we could have the child and then give it up for adoption or an abortion. Both were very difficult choices, to say the least.

Well, we decided on the abortion, believing this was the best thing to do under the circumstances. We made the arrangements; and when the day came, of course, I went with her. That was a rough day. Now, what was done was done; there was no changing it. This created the first actual crack in our marriage.

There was a way of making sure it wouldn't happen again.

For me, a vasectomy at the age of twenty-two would serve as my penances. I gave up being able to create a life because I took one. Even with reducing—no, actually eliminating—the risk of an unwanted pregnancy, my wife had reservations about having sex with me, so my marital sex life went on hold.

1974 Early Summer

I really needed to find a job. Fortunately, instead of becoming someone's employee, I became my own boss, but not in the sheet metal trade. My father came to me with some information about a food manufacturing and distribution company that was selling their employee-operated delivery routes to anyone that had the money to buy a route and a truck, which they would sell from their existing fleet of used ones, to become an independent distributor of the company. It was a franchise, which meant I would own it, buying most of my goods from the company/vendor I bought the route from, but also being able to buy from any another vendors any other products that they did not offer/supply to me. This sounded pretty good to me. It was a one-man operation where I did everything myself: daily customer contact to obtain the resolution of potential or actual problems, of which there were very few; order taking and processing; inventory control; routine scheduling and delivery of products; accounts payable and receivable; designing and printing of the costumer-order forms and new or featured product flyers; and last but not least, the ongoing solicitation of new customers to replace the one lost from time to time.

A lot of work for one man, and it kept me busy most of the time, it's a wonder I had the time and energy for a family or social life of any kind. But I was young and full of hope and pride!

My father loaned me the money to do this, with the promise I would pay him back, which I did within the first nine months of being in business. So on July 4, 1974, Independence Day, I started operating my independent distributorship, with a few weeks of instruction from the employee that was running it for the company. I was now my own boss, the one-man operation in which I called the shots. I buried myself in my business, which took up a lot of my time and energy. This made me too busy and/or too tired to even entertain any thoughts of marital sexual activates, one way for me to cope with my uncomfortable home life. This independent distributorship was to be a temporary situation, because the deal with the company was that I could sell it back to them at any time, keeping in mind the sheet metal trade might have work for me again sometime soon.

Thirty years later, I retired from this supposed temporary independent distributorship, but that's getting too far ahead of myself.

End of Chapter Two

Chapter Three-Part One

New People, Places, and Things

My first year in business was satisfactory. There was a gasoline shortage, so lots of people chose to get their food delivered.

1975 Summer

LITTLE DID I know I would be meeting someone who would spark some huge changes in my life. It was a fellow independent distributor, Denny. We would finish our day's work at about the same time. I would see him at the distribution yard many times. One particular day, neither one of us wanting to go home right away, he suggested we go have a drink together somewhere.

"Sure, but where?" I replied.

"Have you ever been to a strip club?" he asked.

"No, but I would like to see what all the fuss is about," I answered.

So off we went. Inside the club, we sat at a table not too close to the stage where the girls danced.

Onstage was a very attractive young girl. She seemed to be getting a lot of attention from all the men in the place. She finished her set, went offstage, and then another girl came on.

The girl that was performing when we sat down came out from backstage and, to my surprise, came right over to our table.

She leaned down to me and said, "Hi, I'm Cindy. What's your name? May I join you?"

Surprised by this encounter, after a slight hesitation, I answered, "Ya sure, that'd be fine. I'm Jim, this is Denny. Please, sit down,"

then pulled out the chair next to mine for her.

"Thanks, I'll be right back," she responded.

I believe she went to the lady's room. Denny was dumbfounded at what was happening!

"Do you know her?" he asked

"No, I've never seen her before today," I answered.

Denny continued, "Seems you have a way with the ladies. I wonder how you'd do at the Harbor Club on a Friday night."

Needless to say, my ego and curiosity were aroused considerably.

Friday-Night Fever

(◊ *"Who Loves You?"* ◊ *Frankie Valli and the 4 Seasons 1975*)

Okay, after five years of marriage, I suddenly wanted to go out on Friday nights with the guys. I was now living in my basement office, not having any sexual contact with my wife. I knew this wouldn't look good to her.

She would have good reason to be suspicious of my intentions

because something was missing in my married life. Although she would not have sex with me, she still didn't want me having it with someone else.

Very unfair of her, wouldn't you say?

So I just didn't want to come out and say that I was going to or wanted to start doing this. For the next few weeks, I would tell her that Denny kept asking me to go and that I would like to.

She eventually told me, "Then go!"

This was just what I wanted to hear. I called Denny straightaway and told him we're "good to go."

Needless to say, I was quite pleased with the way I handled that. My patience and perseverance paid off, a useful lesson learned.

What to wear? Denny told me a nice shirt and dress pants are good. The next Friday night couldn't come soon enough. Denny came by my house to collect me about 8:00 PM. In his car, he told me the plan. We would go kill some time at a sports bar because it was too early to go to the club; between ten and eleven was a good time to get to the club. You see, by then, the women would have had a few drinks and spent some time with their girlfriends.

Making them more receptive to meeting someone new. Sounded like a good plan; after all, Denny had been doing this for a while now. So why should I question it? Maybe after I got some experience, I could modify it. But for now, that was the plan.

This would be my first time in a nightclub. I'm pleased to report the night went better than expected. At the end of the night, during the ride home, Denny evaluated my first night out, proclaiming,

"You're amazing, a natural. Your first time out and you get three girls' telephone numbers. I didn't get any, and you got three!"

I was hot; the fever had started! This was the wedge that would widen the crack in my marriage.

With little to no attention and/or affection at home, I would now find it someplace else, with someone other than my wife. I continued to go out on Friday nights. The women I met, and may I say there were plenty, didn't thrill me enough to go any further than kissing and playing touchy-feely in the car at the club's parking lot. I've never actually cared for having sex in a car anyway! It was not private enough for me and had too many windows. We started trying some other clubs in the area: smaller, different atmosphere, more intimate and personal.

Still, I wasn't meeting anyone to make me want to get involved. Little did I know, at the time, that a club was not the place I would find her!

1978 Winter

Blizzard of February '78 / Gail

The blizzard of '78 was especially terrible. Twenty-eight inches of snow. My business was not too affected by it. As luck would have it, I didn't lose any days of work.

My truck had gone in the garage for some repairs at the end of the workday that the storm had started on, just before the snow really started to pile up, so it wasn't buried in snow like all the others. Normally, delivery trucks were parked outside at the distribution yard. I would be able to run my business.

Needless to say, my customers were extremely happy to see me because the stores, not being able to get deliveries, had run out of food. For that day,

I was the only one with any supplies. I felt especially needed and important. It's always nice to be needed.

A few days later, things got back to normal. I got back to my routine. Just about every morning before starting my deliveries, I would stop at a favorite coffee shop to get, you guessed it, a cup of coffee.

(◊ "Just the Way You Are" ◊ Billy Joel, 1978)

One very busy morning in February, the coffee shop was extremely crowded. I bumped into someone and knocked their coffee out of their hand. I bent down to pick up the empty cup, and when I stood up, I saw who it was I had bumped into. Feeling badly about this, I offered to replace it.

"Thank you, that would be nice," a female voice answered.

Now seeing who had responded to me, I was delightfully surprised! She was stunning! I hadn't felt this way since the first time I saw Patricia back in 1965.

I had to find out who she was, so I suggested we sit and have our coffee together. She agreed.

We sat and talked. She told me her name was Gail, that she was twenty years old, five feet four inches tall, from out of state, attending a college in the capital city. Gail looked a great deal like Jaclyn Smith a.k.a. Kelly, one of the original "Charlie's Angels," a very popular television show at the time. We lost track of time. She missed her bus to the student teaching job she was headed for, which was in the next town. The next bus would make her too late to go in.

I suggested she spend the day with me on my truck.

"Sounds like fun! Okay, let's go," she replied.

She made a quick phone call from a nearby pay phone, and we were on our way. Gail was to be my second *real* love and my deepest, Patricia being my first.

We had a very enjoyable day together. She got to see what I did for work; and in between my deliveries, we talked, getting to know each other better. She now believed I was trustworthy and agreed we should see more of each other. I purposely failed to say anything about my being married with children. I didn't think it would have gone over too well with her.

You see, my way was not to give information I was not asked for. She never asked if I was married, and I wasn't in the practice of wearing a wedding ring, so she had no reason to suspect that I was.

Gail stayed in the truck while I made the deliveries. I had to keep her away from my customers, them knowing I was married. Things could have gotten said that I wouldn't have wanted her to hear.

My workday was generally about six hours of deliveries and then approximately twenty minutes of paperwork back at the distribution yard office. With the deliveries finished, I took Gail home. She lived in an apartment with two other girls on the outer edge of the capital city. She allowed me to give her a modest kiss good-bye. I told her I would talk to her soon, for she had given me her telephone number.

Okay, now I needed to get more time out of the house. I came up with the idea of playing cards on Tuesday nights with friends from work because card games could last long into the morning hours. My wife didn't seem to mind this. I actually didn't think she would.

A Dream Date

I quietly phoned Gail from my basement office. It was a separate line from the house phone.

No caller ID at this time, thank God.

Made a date with her for the very next Tuesday night; she seemed thrilled. Needless to say, I felt slightly nervous.

Tuesday night arrived. Still feeling a little apprehensive, about seven thirty, I went to pick her up. She greeted me with a very endearing hug and kiss, saying, "Hi, baby, it feels great to see you again."

I melted—you know, like the butter in the hot frying pan!

We went out to eat at a local restaurant. We talked, had a nice meal, and then agreed to get a bottle of wine and to go back to her apartment.

"No one would be home until later, so we could be alone to talk and get to know each other better," she explained.

So back to her apartment we went. Personally, I couldn't wait to be alone with her. I do believe the feeling was mutual.

We started with small talk, and eventually, I took her hand in mine so as to draw her close to me so we could embrace.

Our first intense kiss told me I was in trouble, the kind of trouble you have when you're feeling emotions you really don't have the right to be feeling.

But for me, it had been awhile since I had made love to a woman, so no way was I going to let this opportunity pass me by. She made me extremely excited. Things were getting more passionate by the second. I somehow found the strength to pause for a moment, to ask her if she'd like to go get comfortable.

"Oh ya, I'd love to," she replied. Got up from the couch, saying,

"Wait right here. I'll let you know when I'm ready, okay?" Turned and headed down the hall to her bedroom.

I anxiously agreed, took a large gulp of the wine we were drinking and tried to relax. For you see, our conversation at dinner included likes, dislikes, turn-ons, turn-offs, etc. So without going into too many details, she had a good picture of how I preferred being intimate with a woman.

I do believe she truly wanted to please me as much as I wanted to please her.

She realized my likes, remember Patty with her baby-doll nighties, would be beneficial for both of us.

After about fifteen minutes or so, I heard a soft, sweet voice call to me from her bedroom just a short way down the hallway, like a siren song, "Baby, I'm ready."

I gently replied, "I'm coming, babe!"

My heart was in my throat. I slowly got up from the couch, composed myself, picked up the bottle of wine and glasses. I wanted to be cool, and I didn't want to seem too anxious. After all, other than my wife, Gail would be the first woman I would make love to in quite awhile.

That in itself was stimulating! Our first encounter was all I expected it to be, and more. She's was an incredibly considerate lover, determined to please me in every way. Needless to say, I fell very hard for her.

But if I told her I was in love with her, she would expect more than I could give. Not that I didn't want to; I couldn't. I wanted to continue making love to her forever. If I could have stopped time, I would have.

But everything must come to an end, so you should always cherish beginnings and the time you get to be with someone or to have something you care about that gives a great deal of pleasure.
Because before you know it, it's gone, for whatever reason.

It's a hard lesson to learn—that you don't know what you have until you lose it!

Okay, our first encounter was fulfilled, and I continued holding her in my arms. I do like to kiss and cuddle for a while after making love. I eventually had to tell her I had to leave because I had work in the morning, which I really didn't. I had stopped working on Wednesdays. If I did any work on Wednesdays, it was only paperwork in my basement office, billing and banking stuff, etc.

I would have liked to stay until morning, but not on the first night. I would in time, but I felt I should do this slowly, coming home later and later as time went on. This way, it wouldn't be too much of a shock to my wife.

Gail made my home life easier to tolerate, having a woman who loved and desired me had been absent from my life. She filled a large empty space in my heart. Upon my departure, Gail gave me a long passionate good-bye kiss, told me she loved me!

"Okay I really have to go now. I'll call you later, and I do want us to get together again real soon!" was the best response I could muster.

"Yes, baby, me too, so please drive home safely. Love you!" was her retort.

Baby was what she would call me from that night on; I found it to be very beguiling.

(◊ "She's Always a Woman to Me" ◊ Billy Joel, 1978)

Chapter Three-Part Two

Big City Nights, Big City Lights

(◊"Native New Yorker"◊ Odyssey, 1977)

FOR THE NEXT three months or so, Gail and I would be together on Friday and Tuesday nights. On Friday nights, we would go to the clubs in the capital city for some dancing and then back to her place for making love. Tuesday nights was for being together and doing whatever we felt like and making love. On Tuesdays, I had started to stay with her through the night. She had a part-time job in the capital city, so Wednesday mornings, I would give her a ride to it before I went home.

One unforgettable morning, I awoke to hear crying coming from the kitchen. Puzzled and concerned, I quickly went to the kitchen to find Gail crying because she couldn't fry an egg for me without breaking the yolk. I had told her I liked to dunk toast in the wet yolk, and she always aimed to please me. She kept throwing her failures away.

I hugged her and said, "Don't do that. I'll eat them anyway."

I was sincerely and deeply in love with Gail, and it was getting harder and harder to handle that truth. I guess I was starting to feel guilty every time I left my house to be with her. I would tell myself, *This is not fair to her. So tonight I should tell her the truth that I am married and have two sons*, which, I do believe, would have ended our affair.

However, I would get to her place, and she would greet me with a hug and a kiss, saying, "Hi, baby, I'm so happy to see you again."

I would cave and couldn't do it. I didn't want to lose her. So I would tell myself, *I'll tell her next time, one more night of bliss won't hurt.*

I was so torn between my love for Gail and my love for my sons; I felt that if I left my sons at this time to be with her, they would be too young to understand.

Red in the Window

On the lighter side of things, there is a little incident that I would like to relate to you. One day, on my way back to the distribution yard, I stopped at a square near Gail's house to buy some music—vinyl records, too soon for CDs yet. I noticed in a nearby women's clothing store display window a beautiful red negligee. I called Gail to tell her about it, but she wasn't home. I left a message with one of her roommates, saying, "Please tell Gail to check out the display window of a store named Elaine's on her way home and look for something red."

I was being a little mysterious just to see what would happen. The next time I talked to Gail, which was a few days later, I asked if she had seen what was in the display window at Elaine's. She was very evasive.

"I really haven't had the time to stop and look. So I'll see you Tuesday night?" she asked.

"Of course, I'll be there about eight, okay?" I confirmed.

"That will be fine. I'll make us dinner and a surprise dessert,"
she declared.

I must say, Tuesday night's dinner was good, but the surprise dessert was even better. It was Gail wearing the red negligee from the display window at Elaine's. She looked absolutely incredible! I truly believe my heart skipped a beat!

I couldn't have been more delighted. How could I lose such a treasure like her?

But I did, and to this day, I regret it.

Kelly, Kelly, Kelly!

There is another incident worth mentioning. Gail had told me of a male stalker hiding behind a tree on her street as she made her way home. He would beckon to her in a subdued voice, "Kelllyyyy, Kelllyyyy, Kelllyyyy."

Not knowing her real name, he referred to her as Jaclyn Smith's character, Kelly, from the *Charlie's Angels* television show.

This was real creepy and frightening to her. She didn't know what to do about it. I couldn't be there at the time this would take place, so I did the next best thing that I could think of.

I had a modified .22 caliber starter pistol I kept hidden in the truck because in my business, I handled and carried cash.

I gave it to Gail and instructed her to fire it at the stalker if he came close to her and tried to get physical.

A .22 caliber bullet is not very big or powerful, so it doesn't do a lot of damage. It's been known to bounce off people wearing a heavy coat; so it would take quite a few bullets to kill someone, and at very close range, but it would stun a person long enough to give the victim a chance to get safely away.

Having the gun made her feel safer; thankfully, she never had that confrontation with her stalker. He just, for some unknown reason, stopped. Maybe he saw me with her and that discouraged him from continuing.

Anyway, I told her to hold on to the gun because she felt safer with it than without it. I found out later that letting her hold on to the gun was really not a great idea.

I'll get to why in a minute.

The Easter Bunny Cometh

The Easter holiday was approaching. Gail would be going home to be with her family. She wanted me to go with her, which was impossible for me to do; she would be gone for a week.

I did what I could by taking her to the airport to fly home.

When her flight was called to board, she hugged me and started crying.

I told her, "Just turn around, walk to the boarding area, don't look back, and get on the plane and go, because the sooner you leave, the sooner you'll be back."

I took advantage of Gail's absence and went out with the guys on the following Friday night. They were wondering where I had been and why they had not seen me in awhile. I told them about Gail, which I found out later was a huge mistake. I had forgotten about being discreet. Bad move on my part.

The week she was gone seemed to fly by. When Gail got back, she requested to see more of me, but I wanted to see more of my friends.

I told her from now on, I would spend some time with the guys on Friday nights and then come to see her after.

Does this sound familiar to you?

(◊ "What You Won't Do for Love"◊ Bobby Caldwell, 1978)

She didn't like that arrangement at all, so she showed up where I was hanging out with the guys to be with me. How she found out where I was, I'll never know. Figuring she wouldn't tell me, I didn't ask. Her doing this would make me look whipped and that was something I didn't want anyone to think of me.

I got a little upset and told her, "Please leave. I will see you at your place when I'm done here."

She didn't agree with that.

Not wanting to make a scene, I said, "Okay then, come on. We'll leave right now, together!"

On the ride to her place, I thought to myself, *I can't have her dogging me around like this. She'll get too close and find out the truth.* Also, I really didn't want her to have contact with my friends. So before she could find out the truth, I'd tell her myself.

We pulled up in front of her place, she started to get out, and I said, "Wait, not so fast! There's something you need to be told."

"What's that, I should never do this again?" she sarcastically asked.

"There'll be no need for you to ever do this again because we're finished. It's over, and we can't be together any longer," I explained.

"Why, because of what I did tonight?" she humbly answered.

"No, because I'm . . . I'm . . . married and have two sons,"

I confessed.

There, I finally told her. A great feeling of relief came over me; holding that in had taken its toll on me.

"You're lying!" she wrathfully replied.

"I'm not lying. It's the truth. I wish I could say I'm lying, but I can't," I admitted.

"Well then, if that's the truth," she said as she took out my gun from her pocketbook and pointed it at me, "well, if I can't have you, then no one will!"

I quickly snatched the gun from her hand, saying, "Don't be ridiculous! You're going to shoot me with my own gun, the gun I gave you so you'd feel safe?"

"Jim, baby, I am in love with you," she seductively sobbed. "Stay with me tonight, one last time, please!"

I was astonished by her request!

"No! This has to end now, tonight!" I sternly insisted. "Come on, I'll walk you to your door one last time," trying to be as considerate as I could be.

At her door, she asked me to stay again and again; I refused!

She was holding on to me very tightly and crying.

"I'm not letting go unless you come in and stay with me tonight," she stipulated.

"Please stop this. You're making this harder for me than it is already," I pleaded.

I kissed her good-bye, tasting the salty tears on her lips, and said,

"In the morning, you'll see things more clearly and realize this is the way it has to be. Good night and good-bye. I'm terribly sorry. Please try to find it in your heart to forgive me."

She let go of me, still crying. I quickly got to my car and sped off for home before I had a chance to change my mind.

I was very much in love with Gail, still am today. She didn't realize and may never know how awfully hard it was for me to lose her.

I was truly sorry for all this, and somewhere in my heart, I knew that someday I would get the chance to let her know how I truly felt about her and get the opportunity to make amends. I just didn't think or know it would take as long as it did. So this wasn't quite over yet.

That comes much later, so try to hold on to the thought.

(◊ "Goodbye Yellow Brick Road" ◊ Elton John, 1973)

End of Chapter Three

Chapter Four-Part One

The Rude Awakening

The Telling

(◊ "Baker Street"◊ Gerry Rafferty, 1978)

I AWOKE ON Saturday morning thinking—no, hoping—that the night before was just a bad dream. It wasn't a dream, it really did happen.

Always knew it would, just not when, and I dreaded the thought. The reality of it hit me like a cold slap in the face! I could almost actually feel the sting!

Okay, shake it off. You've been through tougher losses than this,
I told myself then went upstairs to the kitchen for some breakfast.

I ate, very little, got in my car, and drove to my brother's grave site, thinking it would give me some solace. This being the physical representation of a tougher loss in my life. Standing in front of my brother's gravestone, a single tear rolled down my cheek. I was now feeling the heartache of two losses. I really needed to share this with someone, but there wasn't anyone I could go to. I had to try to keep this all inside. But as fate would have it, things would transpired that were going to force me to talk about it.

The following Tuesday night came and went. I didn't go out.

On Wednesday, this sudden change in my habits made Mary curious. She went down to my basement office to ask me,

"Why didn't you go play cards last night?"

"I didn't have the money to waste this week," I explained.

I really wasn't up to going out anyway. I felt I needed a hiatus from the nightlife. Unfortunately, Gail didn't feel that way. She was out there, making contact with my so-called friends, telling them what had happened. Doing her best to turn them against me by telling falsities of how I bad-mouthed them to her. They, believing her, got angry with me; and I heard through the grapevine they were threatening to tell my wife about my affair with Gail.

I decided I would cut them to the quick and tell her myself.

I would rather she heard it from me than from someone else. That way, if someone had approached her with it, she could simply say,

"I already know. Jim told me all about it."

I decided to tell her the very next Saturday. Approaching her, I stated, "There's something I need to tell you, and it's not going to be easy for me. I have been seeing someone, having an affair actually, and yes, I did feel love for this woman. I recently ended it by telling her the truth that I'm married and have two children. To say the least, she didn't take it very well and is trying to stir up trouble for me. So before you hear about it from someone else, I wanted you to hear it from me. I'm very sorry about this, and if you want me to leave, I will."

"I don't want you to leave, but it would be good if you went and stayed at your parents' house for a while," she requested.

Granting her request was the least I could do; so I packed up some things, called my mom, and left, saying, "You'll tell the boys something?"

"I'll tell the boys Nana's not feeling well and you're staying with her to help out for a while," she answered.

"We'll talk about the future of our marriage soon?" I requested.

"Yes, but not too soon. Please, give me some time to absorb all of this," she replied.

I didn't answer her and left. A couple of weeks went by. I heard, once again through the grapevine, that Gail wasn't handling our breakup very well. She went home to her parents' house and tried to end her life by overdosing on drugs. Thank God she failed at the attempt. Her family wanted to know why she would do this. She told them about me: the affair and the breakup. This was her reason for her wanting to kill herself.

Her family was now never going to accept me being with her. I didn't realize this at that time, but this would destroy any chances I would or could have of ever getting back into Gail's life. Nevertheless, if ever I got the chance, I would still try. I never lost hope of reconciling with her. How pathetic is that?

So I carry the proverbial torch for the rest of my life. Talk about paying the piper. I truthfully believe there will always be a considerable degree of love for Gail in my heart until the day I die.

Which Way Now?

I decided the best option left for me was to try my best to get the marriage back in order; I would devote, at least, the next two years of my life to this. There would be no more going out with friends to clubs and things for the time being. If it couldn't be worked out, it would be time to get divorced and a fresh start for any kind of life I could have. I would still be young enough to find some measure of true happiness.

So for the next two years, I strived to be the best husband and father I could be. The father thing came easy to me; I had no problem with that part of it. But no matter how hard I tried, Mary wouldn't warm up to me. I suppose too much had come between us, too much irreparable damage.

Our marriage was totaled. I think we both knew that by now.

We had to stop wasting time and make some changes. I was now very anxious about having someone in my life who loved and desired me. In other words, I desired to be with a woman; it had been a while since I had felt the warmth of another body next to me in bed.

January 1980

Feeling I had done my penance and just about everything I could to repair the marriage, I would now venture out to some places to socialize with people a.k.a. women. Not a nightclub or anything like that. A different approach, like a shopping mall or plaza, knowing lots of women patronized and worked at them. I would get myself back into the swing of things to see if I still had "it." I must say, it worked out better than I expected.

I Love My Mountain Dew

(◊ "Never Too Much"◊ Luther Vandross, 1981)

On a visit to the local mall to buy a pair of socks, hangin' between stores, girl watching, I spied a lovely young woman headed in my direction. In her hand was a can of soda, Mountain Dew to be exact. As she passed across the front of me, I jokingly ask for a sip of her soda. Surprisingly, she stopped, handed me the can, and said, "Sure, here you go."

I thanked her and asked, "So, you here doing a little shopping?"

"No, I work here," she proclaimed.

"And where might that be?" I asked.

"At the shoe store down this way," she pointed out.

"I'm here to buy some socks," I exclaimed.

"Well then, come on down to the shoe store. We have some nice socks, and I'll take care of you," she replied.

Let me stop right here to say she was extremely pretty, with honey blond hair an inch or two below her shoulders, five feet two inches tall and built like a brick s—t house. Think of Christina Applegate / Kelly on the *Married with Children* television show with the body of the British Page Three girl/singer Samantha Fox. A television show character named Kelly. Anything here sound familiar? I had to pursue this one, so to the shoe store I would go.

You want to know her name? Well, so do I. Okay, give me a minute, and I'll get it for both of us. Don't be so impatient. Relax, you gotta be cool with these things, give it a little time, and work up to it. I haven't forgotten how to do this. Wouldn't it be wild if her name's Gail! Okay now, deep breath. Had to be cool about this.

I leisurely made my way to the shoe store so it didn't look like I was chasing her. I think I've still got "it." We'll see in a minute!

Casually entering the store, I stopped and looked around to see where the socks were. The Mountain Dew girl spotted me and signaled me to give her a minute. I could see she was busy with a customer. So I headed over to where the socks were and waited. About a minute or so later, she came over to assist me.

Okay, I'm going to get her name real soon now. Just give me a little more time. You can't rush these things. I don't want to scare her off.

Attending to me, she asked, "Do you see any socks you like?"

"Ya, these look good," I answered.

Noticing they were dress socks, she inquired, "Do you need a new pair of dress shoes to go with those socks?"

"No, all set with shoes, and by the way, my name is Jim," I answered.

"Very nice to meet you, Jim. My name is Maureen," she replied.

Okay, did you get that? What'd I tell you? You gotta be smooth. I haven't lost my touch. Thank God her name wasn't Gail, huh?

Following her to the counter to pay for the socks, I inquired, "So, Maureen, what do you do for fun?"

"I party with my friends and stuff like that," she informed me.

"What would you say to you and me partying together?" I asked boldly.

"Sure, why not? Here's my number. Call me!" she answered.

Okay, let me pause here for a moment to say it's the 1980s, the beginning of a time when it seemed my accelerated life went into hyperdrive. A lot of big changes happened in the eighties, and they seem to have happened extremely fast, which makes my memory a little hazy. There were numerous new people, places, things; and there were women, plenty of women. I could always claim that I refused more women than most men have had. So for the sake of time, I will focus on the ones that had the biggest impact on the life.

Okay, with that being said, I'll get back to my life story.

DeeDee

So I met Maureen on a Saturday and waited until the following Monday night to call her. Remember, I had a telephone in my basement office that was a separate line from the house phone; I still didn't give it out freely. I asked Maureen out for that Tuesday night, knowing this was short notice, but if she said yes, it would answer some questions I didn't want to ask directly. Questions like, is she seeing anyone, and how badly did she want to go out with me?

Pretty clever, wouldn't you say so? I made an art of getting information without asking direct questions. For instance, I would say to a girl I had just met, to find out if she's available,

"So what does your boyfriend think of going out dressed like you are?" because she was dressed rather sexy!

Possible answers would be, "He doesn't mind," or "I don't have a boyfriend."

See what I mean?

THE TIME OF MY LIVES

Anyway, Maureen said yes, gave me her address. I told her I'd be by about 8:00 PM, and we'd go someplace nice for dinner. I was now using the basement door on the side of the house to go in and out, which led directly outside. Also, I had a lot of my clothing in the basement office, so no one knew when I would come and go. My little taste of freedom. I liked it. I was dying to go back to a place where I used to go with Gail. Maybe I could exchange some old memories for some new ones.

After dinner, we went into one of the lounges at the back of the club: soft music, couches, kick your shoes off, really laid-back and comfortable, very relaxed. People would open up and talk uninhibitedly.

I had gotten to know the manager very well. He would allow me to bring in cassette music tapes I had custom-made and play them in the club's sound system. We relaxed, had a drink, and talked about things such as likes and dislikes, turn-ons and turn-offs, etc.; it's best to find these things out in advance of any real sexual contact. I told myself, *I should take it slow with her.* Unknown to her, she could be very helpful to me with the ending of my marriage, someone to be with so as not to be alone. So if I could get something steady going with her, I'd make my move to end my marriage.

"Maureen, do you like this place?" I inquired.

She answered and asked, "Yes, I do very much. You come here often?"

"I used to, but I haven't been here in a while," I confessed. I felt no need to her tell her that I used to come here with Gail.

"Jim, my middle name is Dianne, so if you'd want to call me DeeDee, I'd like that," she requested.

Accommodating her, I inquired, "That's cool. So, DeeDee, do you want to get going soon?"

"Why do you want to go soon?" she asked.

Ah, women. Always answering a question with a question; and if they do give an answer, it's usually a maybe, not a straight yes or no.

"No, we can stay as long you'd like," I declared.

Having no work in the morning, I was not worried about what time I got home. I could just go with the flow. This made me appear single and available.

Sweet freedom. I could get used to this.

Needless to say, our first date went great. When I took her home, she gave me a very affectionate kiss and asked, "When will I see you again? I hope it will be soon!"

"Are you free this coming weekend?" I inquired.

"To go out with you? You bet I am!" she excitedly answered.

"Okay. I'll call you, and we'll talk about it," I exclaimed.

(◊ *"Special Lady"*◊ *Ray, Goodman & Brown, 1979*)

DeeDee and I were spending lots of time together going out to clubs and dinners. Our physical contact was only kissing and hugging in the car when I would take her home. By the way, she lived with her mother, brother, half brother, and her mother's second husband. I made it look like I lived with my mother too. One time, DeeDee had asked me for a phone number so she could call me. She was now under the impression I lived with my mother. I informed her that my mother believed that women who called men, or looked like they pursuing them, were whores, so she dropped the request in fear of my mother thinking that of her. I, living at my mom's house wasn't too far from the truth, because I had made arrangements to move back to my mother's house as soon as possible. I wanted DeeDee to see me do this, so when she'd ask me what I was doing, I'd tell her, "I'm leaving my wife because I want to be with you."

Numerous times, I've told my female fiends that if you meet a married man and he doesn't leave his wife the day after, then he never will.

So one night, before meeting DeeDee after she got out of work, I loaded up my car with a lot of my stuff to take to my mother's house and told Mary I was moving back there until I could find a place of my own because our marriage was finished!

She would have to start looking for a place to live because my parents were none too happy that I wasn't living in the house they owned and bought for me to live in and she was.

"Please tell the boys where I am, and if they need me for anything, to call me there," I requested.

Mary didn't seem to be fazed by this. Her farewell statement made that clear. She exclaimed, "Okay, so just like that, you're leaving? Good. I'll find someone better than you anyway!"

"Knock yourself out. Bye!" I answered her sarcastically.

I don't know why she acted so surprised. This had been coming for a while. I now wish I had done this when Gail was still in my life.

By the way, Mary never did find that someone, but that's her story. She'll have to write or tell that herself.

My car trunk and backseat were loaded with my stuff.

I sat on a bench in the mall, just outside the shoe store, waiting for DeeDee to finish her work shift, thinking about what was happening, and telling myself that no matter how this went, I'd have to live with it. This was only the beginning of some enormous changes in my life. It was a little scary!

DeeDee came out from the store, saw me sitting on the bench looking rather sad, and asked, "Hey, lover, why so sad?"

Answering her, I said, "Come on, babe, there is something you need to see!"

We left the mall, got to my car, I opened her the door, she got in, I walked around the back to get to my door. She would always lean over and unlock my door for me.

By the way, that's a really big sign that a woman really likes you.

As I got in, she noticed all the stuff and asked, "What's all this?"

referring to all my stuff in the backseat. Taking her hand in mine, I said, "I have genuine feelings for you, and I think you feel the same way toward me too. I've been wrestling with making a really big decision in my life. The feelings I believe we have for each other helped make it for me, so please understand changes like this don't happen overnight. I have left my wife tonight so we can be together. I know I didn't tell you I was married. You never asked. I'm sorry for this being so sudden. I wanted you to see me do this, to show you that my feelings for you are genuine, and I'm not just stringing you along."

She leaned over, hugged, and kissed me, saying, "I am in love with you, Jim, and now I know for sure that I want you to be the first man I have sex with."

A virgin! Oh great, more pressure!

Now I wondered how old she really was. She had told me she was nineteen, soon to be twenty. Now I'm thinking she's younger, but I'll leave that for later.

"I need to get this stuff to my mom's house. Would you come and help me?" I asked her.

"Of course, I will, lover!" she answered.

Lover. I liked that; it had a very endearing feel to it.

We put my stuff in the basement; I would sort it out tomorrow.
Mom must have heard us. She came down to the basement and asked if I was okay, with all that was happening. She also asked who DeeDee was. I told her she's a very special person in my life. I do believe they both knew that I meant.

We finished up and went someplace local to relax and have a drink.

She was never asked for an ID when with me. She liked that a great deal.

I wanted to ask her about me being her first, but I let it lie for now.

"So what are we doing this weekend?" she asked me.

"What would you like to do?"

Answering a question with a question. Yeah, sometimes we men do that also.

She requested, "I'd like for us to go someplace where we can be alone together all night."

"You mean to have se—I mean, make love?" I asked.

"Yes, you okay with that, lover? You seem a bit nervous," she inquired.

"Me, nervous? Nah. Ya, I'm okay with it." Then I suggested, "I could get us a room for a night at a local motel. Is that what you mean?"

"Yes, I'll need to do a little shopping before we do this," she informed me.

A Dream in Sheer Violet

(◊ *"(Let's Go) All the Way"* ◊ The Whispers)

It was her first time, and first times are always scary. She had gone into the bathroom to change into what she had bought for this occasion.

My third time with a virgin: Patricia, Mary, and now DeeDee made three. No brag, just fact.

I knew to be patient, gentle, and to create a relaxed atmosphere: soft music, wine, and candles always created the right mood.

She was in the bathroom for a while, so I gently knocked on the door and asked, "You okay in there, babe?"

"Yes, lover. I'm not sure I like how I look in this," she replied.

"Let me have a look so I can give you my thoughts, so come out and try some of the wine we got to see how you like it," I suggested, trying to make her feel relaxed.

The door opened very slowly, and she stepped out, dressed in a beautiful and sexy sheer and lace violet baby-doll nightie.

I silently gasped and lovingly proclaimed, "Wow! You look like a dream!"

(◊ "*For Your Eyes Only*"◊ Sheena Easton)

Making love to her was heavenly bliss. She told me she had had a dream of someone that looked like me being her first, so I guess her dream came true. Intimacy with her made me feel loved and desired again and gave me the strength to handle everything that was coming in the near future. Hopefully, she'd be right there by my side, but there were no guaranties of that, so I'd have to take my chances.

As it turned out, DeeDee was seventeen, soon to be eighteen in late autumn, which made me ten years older than her. That night was the first of many bliss-filled nights like that.

Meanwhile, Mary filed for State welfare aid and got it. I was called in to arrange my child-support payments to the State welfare department. In all the time I paid, I never missed once. Prearranged visiting rights with my sons for me were every other weekend.

Procedures had to be followed for getting divorced in my State. I would file for a separation, Mary would then file a restraining order on me, which was later extended to both of us. Filed for a divorce, which I filed a no-fault, and Mary counterfiled with cruel and abusive—her lawyer's idea.

I contested that, so it went back and forth for a while. Mary's lawyer had ideas that were not going to work. It took about five years to iron this out and get into court. But there were things that happened during that time that changed the outcome of the divorce. Also, Mary's lawyer delaying things didn't help her argument. As I tell my story, it will be made clear.

So DeeDee and my sons were getting to know each other, and they got along great. The summer of 1980 seemed to fly by, spending time with DeeDee. My sons would be with us on the odd weekends.

Chapter Four-Part Two

New Place, Little Space

1981 Spring

I HAD FINALLY found an apartment I could afford in the next city east of mine, a building on a dead-end street with four units, where I got a first-floor, three-room, one-bathroom apartment. I moved in as quickly as I could with DeeDee. As it turned out, her mother didn't live too far away from us; she liked that. We went through the winter together; our first Christmas was really something special.

The apartment was small, which probably contributed to the growing tension between us; and with the divorce taking so long to happen, DeeDee was getting impatient.

Youth doesn't seem to want to wait long for things to happen, although they are young and have plenty of time.
Yeah, I should talk, huh?

She was feeling that I wasn't going to go through with the divorce and would go back to my wife. I reassured her that any feelings I had for my soon-to-be-ex-wife were dead; it was her that I loved and wanted to be with now. Even still, she started to spend more and more time at her mother's house—her attempt at trying to speed things up. But there wasn't anything I could do to make things go any faster. The tension grew. We started to have arguments over the littlest things, and this was not the way I wanted to live, loving her as much as I did.

I suggested, "If you're so unhappy living here with me, then, as much as I don't want you to, maybe you should go back to your mother's house."

The next day, while I was at work, she left; but strangely enough, she kept her keys to the apartment. I wasn't happy with her being gone, but you can't force people to do what they don't want to.

(◊ "Aint No Sunshine"◊ Bill Withers)

1981 Summer

With DeeDee now gone, I had some free time on my hands. What to do with this time? I wanted to do something that would maybe make my life better, so I decided to extend my education and take some night classes in a subject I had an interest in, which was technical illustrating. One of the colleges in the capital city had some night courses, so I signed up and started as soon as I could.

So I was living on my own, running my business during the day, going to school two nights a week, seeing my sons every other weekend. I definitely needed some fun in my life—you know, all work and no play . . . So in the autumn, I decided to go out and do some clubbing again and see what excitement I could find. I was ready for anything. I would return to the place where Gail and my last night started; you know how it ended. I was sure things had changed there. The building known as the Castle Club Complex in a suburb city north of me now had three different clubs in it. That's where I would go and check things out to see what action I would find.

Once again, things worked out better than I expected.

Enter Linda

*(◊ **"Take on Me"** ◊ a-ha)*

At the club, I ran into Angela, a female friend of mine I hadn't seen in a while. She was very happy to see me and to find out that I was available because she had a friend she wanted me to meet. That friend was Linda.

"Okay, where is she?" I inquired.

"She's on the dance floor. She'll be back when she's finished," Angela informed me.

"Well, it would be good to have a drink here for her when she returns. What's she drinking?" I asked.

"I'll tell the bartender to give us another round," Angela answered.

"And I'll take care of it," I insisted.

"Thank you, that's very nice of you. Linda will appreciate the drink after dancing," she gratefully said.

I had to inquire, "Angela, what does Linda look like?"

"Jim, I know what you like. Trust me, you'll like Linda," she assured me.

No sooner did she finish her statement than Linda showed up.

Angela made the introduction, "Linda, I would like you to meet a friend of mine, Jim."

"It's nice to meet you, Jim," Linda greeted.

Linda was about five foot four, shoulder-length dirty-blond hair. Reminded me of Olivia Newton-John. She was nineteen, soon to be twenty.

She lived with her parents and four sisters, so any intimacy would have to happen at my place.

"Jim, do you dance?" Linda inquired.

I have failed to mention that I am one hell of a dancer, if I do say so myself. To be popular with the ladies, you really had to be because if it's one thing women like, it's to dance with a man they're attracted to. For them, it's like having sex without really having sex—you know, the foreplay before the actual foreplay!

"I would love to dance with you, Linda," I informed her.

"Good, as soon as I cool down, we dance!" she decreed.

We danced, had a real good time together, spent the rest of the evening in each other's company. At the end of the night, we exchanged phone numbers so we could make contact and arrange to go out soon.

I walked her to Angela's car. We kissed passionately good night. I called her a few days later, and we arranged a date. We went out for dinner. After dinner, I asked her what she'd like to do.

She replied and asked, "I'd like to see your apartment, if that's okay with you?"

I thought to myself, *That's more than okay with me*, and answered her, "Sure, that'd be great. I've got a really fine bottle of wine, and we could sit back and relax, get to know each other better."

Our first encounter was not as romantic as I would have liked it to be. I think we were both starving for affection. So it was more of a hot and heavy encounter, but still some good lovin'.

Yes, we made love on our first date! This was not an uncommon occurrence for me! Again, no brag, just fact.

Living at home with her parents, she could not stay out all night. She was expected to be home between 2:00 and 2:30 AM. So after we made love, I'd have to take her home. Our relationship flourished.

We spent lots of time together with and without my sons, which Linda liked very much. The feeling was mutual, thank God!

1982 Spring

Linda liked my little place, although I was in the process of moving back to the marital home my parents owned. I told Linda everything that was going on in my life. Like I had informed my soon-to-be-ex-wife, Mary, that my financial situation was in rough shape, which meant I needed to get back to what I considered to be my home. Mary protested. I told her she needed to leave or my parents would evict her, but not my sons; they could stay, to which there were no objections from anyone. Gave her a date—three weeks prior to my moving back in.

Unknown to me, two days before the day I was to move back in, she had taken the boys and left.

Where to? I didn't know and wouldn't find out for about a year or so. I did not see my sons in all that time and still kept up with paying my child support. Mary was telling them I was some kind of monster, and they should not have contact with me.

Linda and I arrived at the house in my delivery truck, full of my stuff, to no one living there. Mary had only taken hers and the boys' clothing. Everything else was there. Thank God, because I didn't have the money to replace what I had left behind. Linda liked this place even better than my other place. After all, this place was bigger. Good, because she would be spending a lot more time there with me. Our relationship was growing.

The Bachelor's Life for Me!

1982 Summer

Meanwhile, in the back of my mind, DeeDee was still out there, and we had never officially said good-bye; but I couldn't worry about that now. I had bigger things worrying me. Like not knowing where my sons were and not seeing them, which bothered me immensely.

The divorce procedures were dragging along slowly. That and not seeing my sons made me want to talk to my lawyer, Bob. I called him and told him what was going on. He told me, "Come by my office tomorrow afternoon and we will talk about it. Believe it or not, what your wife is doing is going to work in our favor. Don't worry about it. I now see that if we give her enough rope, she'll hang herself. See you tomorrow. Bye."

Bob consoled and counseled me, saying "Jim, I know what you're feeling, but if you do the wrong thing now, it won't help our argument in court when we get there. And we will get there, so please do as I tell you."

Which was to keep paying the child support, go have some fun, and live the bachelor's life I had missed out on because before I knew it, my sons would be back in my life, big-time.

I took Bob's advice, and my apartment became the place to be after hours, an after-hours party every weekend.

Home video games were the rage, so I made the backroom, off the kitchen, a game room; needless to say, it was the most popular room in the house.

(◊ "Steppin' Out"◊ Joe Jackson)

End of Chapter Four

Chapter Five-Part One

The Revolving Door of Life

(◊"And the Beat Goes On" ◊ The Whispers)

1983 Spring

THERE NOW APPEARED to be a revolving door on my apartment and in my life. Moving back to my hometown felt great. It's the closest I ever came to going home again; I would have this feeling quit a bit in the future.

Ah! The future, it comes up quick. Sometimes, when you're not looking, it can pull the rug out from under you. Anyway, I was home. I think I now know how Dorothy and Toto must have felt returning home from Oz.

Let me get you caught up a bit. Just before moving back to what I considered my home, I had finished my night classes, but never got the chance to put them to any use.

My place was quite the hot spot, the after-hours place to be, hence the revolving door. Linda liked it at first, but seemed to tire of it after a while. Luckily, most of my visitors/guests were trustworthy; actually most of them were women, a good time all around, have to say for myself.

1983 Summer

Ghost at My Door

(◊"Total Eclipse of the Heart"◊ Bonnie Tyler)

Linda's job was in the capital city, and she lived in a coastal city. Therefore, she found it easier after work to come to my house, which was only five miles north of the capital city. We would do stuff, and then I'd take her home later. She would usually arrive at my place about 6:00 PM. I would get home about 4:00 PM, giving me time to get cleaned up and chill out before Linda arrived. On one momentous day, at about 5:00 PM, my doorbell rang. I couldn't imagine who it might be. Went to answer the door, filled with curiosity. Opening the door, I heard a voice I thought I'd never hear again.

"Hello, lover, how've you been? Miss me?"

Yeah, it was DeeDee. Needless to say, I was caught off guard; the rug got pulled from under me.

"How did you know I had moved back here?" I asked.

"Well, silly, my keys no longer worked at the other place, and you had mentioned, more than once, about getting back here. So I made the assumption you had got yourself back here. So how about we go for an early dinner?" she requested.

"Well, I . . . I . . . I . . . can't right now. You'll have to give me a rain check," I nervously replied.

"Ya, sure, lover. What's your phone number here?" she inquired.

"That's all right, DeeDee, I still have your mother's phone number. You are still living there, right?" I replied tensely.

"Yes, I am, lover, so don't make me wait too long," she insisted.

"No, I won't. I'll be in touch real soon." I hastily replied.

For you see, it was almost time for Linda to arrive, and not really knowing DeeDee's intentions, I didn't want to jeopardize my relationship with Linda, so I had to get DeeDee to leave. We were talking at the front door, so I stepped out on the porch to walk her to her car and see her off. No sooner did she pull away than Linda came walking around the corner.

Greeting her, I gave her a kiss and stated, "Hi, babe, how was your day?"

"It was okay, you know, hun, same old same old!" she answered.

"Ya, are you hungry?" I inquired.

"A little," she responded.

"Okay then, let's go eat," I implied.

"Jim, I do need to freshen up first," she stated.

"Of course, babe, just let me know when you're ready to go. I'll be in the game room," I instructed.

I don't think she sensed my nervousness. She went into the bathroom, I into the kitchen, breathed a sigh of relief and thought to myself, *That was close, too close for comfort.*

Continuing in my thoughts, I supposed DeeDee wanted to be back in my life, but I wasn't sure of that. Usually, it's one door closes, another one opens, but I've got two doors open. One will have to be closed soon. Seems it's to be feast or famine. What to do? Shelf it for now; I'll give it more thought later.

I now had to find out what DeeDee was up to. As I stated before, Linda wasn't able to stay overnight; so on Fridays, she wouldn't come to my place after work. That made Friday nights mine to do with whatever I wanted. A good opportunity to get with DeeDee. Called her to make a date. She was very agreeable. We went out to dinner.

At dinner, I had to use my unique way of getting answers without asking direct questions. With dinner ordered, I poured the wine and began the Q and A.

"How've you been?" I asked directly. "You look great!" Complimenting her.

"Thank you, I've been okay," she replied.

"Surely you been going out having fun!" I stated.

"Oh ya, I've been out, but something always seems to be missing," she informed me.

"What do you believe that something is?" I playfully inquired.

I was being reserved, wanting her to give me a straight answer. With very little hesitation, she stated, "Don't be silly. You know as well as I do, it's you."

"Do you have any idea what you'd like to do after dinner?" I asked, still being demure.

"Well, lover, I will need to stop by my mother's so I can get a few things that I'll need to stay with you at your place overnight. After all, I'd like to see the inside. The other day, when I was there, you didn't ask me in, and you kind of rushed me off," she stated. "Do you have something to hide, lover?"

Still being demure, I answered, "Me, something to hide? Not at all. You want to see the apartment, you will."

I had anticipated this and put away any sign of Linda, which was actually very little. Also felt a little guilty hiding from DeeDee that there was someone in my life. But like I said before, not knowing her true intentions, I didn't want to jeopardize what I had going with Linda at this time.

If DeeDee was serious about coming back into my life, I would have to do something about Linda, but not until I was sure about DeeDee.

THE TIME OF MY LIVES

A man can only juggle multiple women for so long.

Best-Laid Plans of . . .

As it turned out, DeeDee did want to be back in my life, but I wasn't going to let this happen overnight. I would play it out for all it was worth. I would use the summer of 1983 to phase Linda out and let DeeDee in. I set a potential deadline to be sometime before my birthday, in the fall, for obvious reasons.

Often, I would go to Linda's workplace and take her out for lunch. A few times, one of her coworkers, Janet, would come with us. I liked Janet, I found her to be very attractive. She reminded me of a young Shirley MacLean, only with black hair.

One of the times that the three of us were at lunch, Linda left the table to use the lady's room, Janet took this opportunity to ask me if I knew anyone who sold cocaine. Taking this as an opportunity to get her phone number for future reference, I told her, "I might, so give me your number. I'll call you as soon as I know. Let's not say anything to Linda, okay?"

She agreed, we finished our lunch, they went back to work, and I went on my way, thinking, *If things don't work out with DeeDee, then maybe I could get something going with Janet.* Soon after this, I started to be less and less available to Linda. I had started to phase her out of my life. A few days later, I called Janet to tell her I had located what she wanted, and if she could meet me for a drink somewhere, I would deliver it to her. She entirely agreed. This would be the first of several encounters with her. I guess you could say I had three women in my life; it wouldn't be the last time.

1983 Late Summer

A Reunion of Sorts

It had now been about a year and a half since I had seen or talked to my sons. In late August, on a Sunday, I had taken the day to be alone and get some downtime, relaxing in front of the television, when the phone rang. I answered it and, to my pleasant surprise, heard the voice of my eldest son, Jim. He was a little hysterical. I asked him to calm down and tell me what had happened. I was thrilled to hear from him, even under distressed circumstances.

He related to me that he and his mother had had a fight, and he ran out to call me. It was almost lunchtime, so I suggested I come and get him and we'd go to lunch to talk about this incident.

After Jim told me that he and his mother had had a disagreement on something, I decided to call Mary to let her know he was with me.

I was a very surprised by her response, which was, "I knew he'd call you!"

I suggested he stay with me for a while until they both calmed down and could work this out.

Her response was, "You can have him. Come get his clothes. I don't want him here."

I replied, "Wait a minute. Do you realize what you're doing?"

Jim then directed me to where they were living to get his things. We arrived to find some green trash bags full of his clothes on the front porch of the house. They were living in the fourth floor apartment. Stepping into the front hall, there was a central staircase. I could hear Mary up on the fourth floor outside her apartment.

I called to her, saying, "Mary, do you realize what you are doing?"

"Just take him and his clothes and go!" was her answer.

"Mary, you're making a big mistake!" I proclaimed.

No reply. I heard her door close, so we left. On the ride to my place, I reassured him that everything would be all right. "She'll calm down and want you to come back."

"I don't want to go back there. I want to stay with you, Dad," he proclaimed.

Dad. No one had called me that in awhile. It felt really good.

Jim ended up staying with me. His younger brother, Vincent, followed about two months later. They now lived with me, right up to the divorce and beyond. I will relate later how they were with me after the divorce. When things calmed down, I insisted the boys see their mother. Every other weekend was the plan. Mary agreed to that.

With my sons living with me now, something had to change. No more after-hours parties. I wasn't going out to the clubs as much anyway, so it wasn't happening as much anymore. Also, had to contact my lawyer to tell him what had happened and get welfare to stop my child-support payments.

I wouldn't have time for multiple women, Linda and DeeDee, with my sons in my life. So at least one woman had to go. It would be Linda. I would keep my verbal contact with Janet and maintain status quo.

DeeDee had been a little curious why I wasn't more available for her, surmising I had someone in my life, and for that time being, Linda was. And now, so were my sons. Knowing DeeDee would not mind my sons being in my life made her the obvious choice. Not that Linda minded my sons being around; they just preferred DeeDee to Linda.

I had already figured a way to fix all this.

(◊"Turn Your Love Around" ◊ George Benson)

Exit Linda, Re-Enter DeeDee

1983 Early Autumn

There was a favorite family vacation place to the south I hadn't been to in quite awhile. Knowing Linda could not go there with me for a weekend, I told her I was going with some of my friends. Of course, I knew DeeDee could and would love to go with me.

I planned to go on the four-day Columbus Day weekend. It would be one of the weekends the boys would be with their mother.

DeeDee and I were to leave on the Friday evening and return the following Monday night. She packed at her mother's house and would call me when she was ready for me to come pick her up so we could, then head south for the long weekend.

Having some time to kill, I called Linda at her work to say good-bye before I left for the weekend. She told me she felt bad that she couldn't go with me and related that it would a long while before she could do anything like that. So if I wanted to do stuff like that, maybe she and I shouldn't see each other anymore. The good-bye went further than I thought it would, but that's okay. I rather she felt she broke up with me than I with her. That worked out better than if I had planned it!

No sooner had I hung up from Linda than a car horn sounded. The boys' mother had come to get them for the weekend. Got the boys on their way. I had already packed my stuff and put them in my car. Just as things calmed down, the phone rang; it was DeeDee calling to tell me she was ready for me to pick her up.

(◊"I'm So Excited" ◊ The Pointer Sisters)

Just as we arrived at the resort I had made reservations for, it started to rain and continued to until Sunday. So for the first two days, we stayed in our room and made love till it hurt, ordered out for food and drink. Mid-Sunday afternoon, the sun showed itself, so we ventured out to see what fun we could find. Remember, I had been to this area before. Although it had been awhile ago, I recalled quite a lot.

As we drove around, stopping here and there at places that sparked our interest, one in particular was a little lingerie shop in a small mall on the main street of the main town of the area. On the way back to the resort, we spotted a very romantic-looking waterfront restaurant. DeeDee asked if we could have dinner there later. I agreed, went in, and made a reservation. With that set, we continued back to our accommodations to chill out and get dressed for dinner. DeeDee wore a very form-fitting black-and-white evening gown that wrapped in front, with a low-cut neckline. She looked incredibly sexy.

We had a window table overlooking the water. It had a very romantic atmosphere, and DeeDee was particularly pleased with this. After dinner, I ask DeeDee what she would like to do.

She requested, "I would like for us to go back to the resort so I could go for a swim in the pool that's just outside our room, and then I will put on that sexy lingerie you bought me today and go crazy on you."

(◊"Rock Steady" ◊ The Whispers)

It was purely one of those weekends that I, if I could, would have stayed in for the rest of my life, a futile attempt at freezing time.

If you've ever had an encounter of extreme bliss, then you know what I'm talking about!

Monday came sooner than we would have liked. We needed to head home by late afternoon. On the ride home, DeeDee informed me she had packed more than she needed for the weekend because her plan was to move in with me and my sons. After a weekend of love and romance, I was very agreeable. I knew the boys would not mind at all; they were both very fond of her.

It had all the warm feelings of a family atmosphere until something horrendous happened to destroy what we had forever!

Chapter Five-Part Two

An Unforgivable Invasion

1984 Late Spring

MY PARENTS HAD sold my childhood home and moved to an apartment complex in the next city to the north. My father had a truck he used for his work, and having moved to a place with no place to park it, he would now park it in one of the garages in the back of the house where I lived.

The day of the shocking event began on a bright Sunday morning. The boys were with their mother for the weekend and would be back in the evening. DeeDee and I were seated at the kitchen table having breakfast. My father showed up to get something from his truck and stopped in to say hello, innocent enough for now. I received a phone call from a friend in need of my help for a couple of hours; so I agreed to help him, said my good-byes, and left.

Left my father and DeeDee at the house with no thoughts of mistrust for either one of them. I returned to find that my father had left and DeeDee was relaxing in front of the television. The day went on with no inkling that anything erroneous had happened, DeeDee and I went out for dinner, which was pleasant enough, but I had a strange feeling that something was bothering her.

So I asked if anything was wrong. She answered, "No, nothing's wrong."

Typical answer when there really is something wrong.

She was acting very uneasy as though something had happened, and she was trying real hard to hide it. I knew her signs when she had something bothering her and was trying to keep it from me.

That worked only for so long, for you see, she generally concealed nothing from me. I knew sooner or later she'd tell me, so I didn't push it. We left the restaurant. No sooner did we get into the car than she started crying. My first concern was if she was in some sort of pain.

She calmed down enough to tell me that she was not in pain. That was good, but I needed to know why she was crying, so I asked,

"Sweetheart, what's wrong?"

She took a moment to compose herself and then started to tell me something that in my wildest dreams I could not have imagined would or could ever have happened. I know now how hard it was for her to tell me.

She began, "Jim, after you left this morning, your father tried to have sex with me. I fended him off as best I could by turning my back to him. He groped me with one hand and relieved himself with the other, then quickly left, threatening me so I wouldn't tell you."

My stomach started to feel very tight, and a wave of nausea overtook me. I quickly opened my door and proceeded to vomit my dinner right there in the parking lot. Went back inside the restaurant to clean up in the men's room, returned to the car and told her not to worry about him doing anything to hurt her and asked if she was okay staying at the house tonight and told her I would fully understand if she wanted to stay at her mother's house for the night.

"As long as you are with me, I'll be okay!" she firmly stated.

I believed every word she said about what had happened. I just had a problem believing that my own father could do something like this to her and me—yes, to me. I felt a sacred trust had been violated. I mean, if you can't trust your own father, who can you trust?

I would have to confront him with this right away. Wanting to avoid any physical confrontation, I decided to call him on the phone. So Monday, late afternoon, before DeeDee arrived home from work, I called my parents' home.

My mother answered, "Hello?"

"Hi, Mom. Is Dad there?" I asked her.

"Yes, he is," she declared and then asked. "Is there something wrong at the house?"

"No, not with the house, but there is a problem between me and Dad," I informed her.

I really didn't want to get my mother involved. But I had to say something.

"Dad did something unforgivable, and I need to talk to him about it. So please, put him on the phone."

She called to him, saying, "Joe, your son, Jim, is on the phone."

He took the phone and greeted me, "Hello, Jim."

I started by saying, "Dad, DeeDee told me what happened Sunday morning, and the only thing that is stopping me from coming after you and breaking your legs is the fact that you're my father!"

His reply was, "I don't know what you're talking about. Nothing happened!"

Not to my surprise, he denied anything had taken place, so I pressed him, "Don't try to deny what happened. She told me and I believe her," I rebuked. Then I related to him what DeeDee had told me.

His answer to my claim was, "Ya, so? It was nothing. I mean, she's only a woman. It's no big deal."

I was infuriated and replied, "No big deal! No big deal! What you've done is unforgivable. Don't set foot in my apartment ever again. I want nothing to do with you, I don't want to see or talk to you. You disgust me. I'm ashamed that you're my father. And stay away from DeeDee, or I will forget you are my father and come after you."

He then passed the phone to my mother, saying, "Here, talk to your son. He's talking and acting crazy!"

"Jimmy, what's going on? What has happened?" she inquired.

I told her some of what had happened. I felt she needed to know something. I knew she wouldn't want to believe it, but she knew what her husband was capable of.

I ended the call with "I love you, Mom. I will talk to you soon. Bye."

Returning my sentiment, she replied, "I love you too, son. Try not to be too upset. Bye."

And we each hung up the phone.

DeeDee appeared about thirty minutes later. I greeted her with a kiss and an "I love you," and told her that I talked to my father.

"You have nothing to worry about. I will make sure nothing like that ever happens again, so please try to stop being nervous and afraid. He's not going to do anything to you because you told me about it," I assured her.

"I will try," she replied.

Try as she did, she couldn't get past it; so like a cancer, it ate away at our relationship and eventually caused us to break up again. And I should add, for the last time!

1984 Midsummer

Exit DeeDee, Enter Janet

DeeDee found it very uncomfortable to live or be at my place.

She decided to go back to her mother's. I wasn't happy with this, but like I said before, you can't force someone to do what they don't want to.

I had kept in touch with Janet, just in case DeeDee left me again, and was I glad I did. I had never told her about DeeDee, so as far as she knew, Linda and I had broken up about six months ago and I hadn't been seeing anyone. Knowing she and her boyfriend had broke up a few months ago, I figured I'd ask her out to dinner to see if I could get with her.

A Perfect First Date

(◊"The Look of Love" ◊ ABC)

She agreed to my invite and accompanied me out to dinner. We got along famously. Prior to going out with her, I found out what her favorite wine was; so on the night of our date, I picked up a bottle, arrived early so we could sample it.

The wine, you see, was the means to get me back into my date's dwelling later to have a nightcap with her. It seemed to work every time!

At dinner, we chatted about why we hadn't done this sooner.

We both came to the same conclusion that it was timing, and timing was everything. Finished dinner, left the restaurant, got to my car. I asked her, "Would you like go on to someplace?"

To my surprise, her reply was, "No, I'd like for us to go back to my place and have some more of that awesome wine you brought over."

To my pleasant surprise, she had beaten me to the punch!

Stolen my thunder, but I didn't mind at all.

I wholeheartedly agreed with her request, and back to her place we went. Her taking charge like that was really a turn-on for me. I like a woman that knows what she wants and goes for it. We had the wine and each other. She slipped into something sexy, long, black, lacy, and sheer. We made love like two people who were extremely hungry for some real affection. Out of that lovemaking, a relationship was born.

My sons very quickly had a fondness for Janet, which was always an important thing.

(◊"On the Loose"◊ Saga)

Not to my knowledge, Janet's ex-boyfriend wanted her back. I found this out soon enough and very awkwardly. Janet went with her parents to a lakefront summer cottage up north that they had rented for two weeks. Not wanting to stay for the two weeks, Janet invited me and my sons to come on the Sunday of the second week to spend the day with them and then bring her home. Janet didn't have a car of her own.

When we arrived at Janet's apartment, her ex-boyfriend was waiting on the front steps. I confronted him and told him Janet didn't want him there and if he didn't leave, she'd go to one of her neighbors and call the police.

Note: We didn't have cellular telephones at that time.

Not wanting that kind of trouble, he left. With my sons there, I was glad this situation didn't get out of hand—you know, get physical in any way. Janet was too. I got her luggage out of my truck and took it in her place; she seemed a little shaken by what had happened. I tried to comfort her with a kiss and a hug and told her I needed to get the boys home and would call her later. Off we went. I was thinking to myself what the hell was going to happen now.

Janet and I were getting along really good, and now a wedge had appeared that might possibly split us up.

1984 Autumn

Two Ships

Our weekend practice was on Friday nights, we would go our separate ways—she out with her friends and I with mine. On Saturday nights, we would be together.

As fate would have it, I went to a club in the capital city and met Deidre. She was five feet eight inches tall—a good height for a model, which she was at the time—very pretty, with shoulder-length dirty-blond hair, appearing to be a combination of Michelle Pfeiffer and Cameron Diaz in looks. Plain to see why she was a model.

It was a brief encounter that would spark future interests. For you see, although she told me she was on a date, that didn't stop her from giving me her phone number and requesting me to call her sometime. Finding her very attractive, I jumped at the opportunity to have a line of communication with her and happily took her number for future reference. After all, I was still seeing Janet, but the question was, for how much longer?

Set aside Deidre in your memory for later.

Janet and I were doing okay for the time being, but I felt her ex-boyfriend was trying very hard to get back in her life. An ex-boyfriend always has a slight advantage because they have already made a place for themselves in a woman's heart and a history.

Opening a familiar door was always easier than opening an unfamiliar one.

(◊"True"◊ Spandau Ballet)

Janet didn't say anything, but I knew her ex was trying to work his way back to her. The truth was she was considering taking him back. I could feel a distance growing between us, and wasn't sure what to do about it or if I wanted to. I did like Janet very much, and I felt, given the right nurturing, it could have grown into a true love between us.

But her ex-boyfriend was barking at the door, literally. More than once, he had shown up at her front door while I was there. At her request, I'd let her handle it, unless he got unruly; and only then would I step in. Fortunately for him, that never happened. Knowing that our relationship was under a stern, I had to think of myself, because if she went back to him, I'd be with no one; and after what I had been through recently, I didn't want that to be alone at this time.

In my attempt to have someone to fall back on, I kept in touch with Deidre as much I could without making her think I was interested in her enough to ask her out. Sort of keeping her at arm's length.

Exit Janet, Enter ????

It was becoming clear to me that Janet was really thinking of taking her ex-boyfriend back; all the signs were there. It got to the point where I needed to know where I stood, so I gently confronted her with it.

The major holidays were approaching, and I wanted to know if she would be in my life for them. I have mentioned before the signs, which were that she became somewhat aloof and not as affectionate—the true signs of someone wanting to make changes. I realized that she would be leaving me soon, thinking that this could be the last Saturday night with her. These nights were usually us going out for dinner and then going back to her place to make love. I was still a bit uncomfortable about having a woman stay overnight with me at my house.

(◊"Lady Love Me (One More Time)"◊ George Benson)

If this was to be our last Saturday night together, and I had a strong feeling it was, I really wanted it to be special and somewhat unforgettable; so I took her to a very nice restaurant in the capital city. The night went as I had anticipated, so in the morning, I said my good-byes, telling her I would miss her.

I left, wondering what to do now. The answer seemed to be obvious. Pursue Deidre!

End of Chapter Five

Chapter Six-Part One

Running Around Again

1984 Late Autumn

PURSUE DEIDRE? I decided I would need to give this idea more thought.

I had just come out of another failed relationship, did I really want to even try right now to get into another?

So I wouldn't expect to have a relationship with Deidre. I would just turn it up a notch and see what happened. Deidre was a very attractive woman. I'm sure she had quite a few men pursuing her, so I wouldn't get my expectations up too high. The last thing I needed right now was another disappointment.

After giving this venture as much consideration as I felt it needed, I decided to try to find out if she was even interested in going out with me. I would have to be tactful and not reveal an interest in something that might not even exist. My first earnest, majestic effort at being the careful man.

Well, my initial result failed. She didn't actually refuse me; she just told me, "Not right now, Jim. I'm very busy with the modeling career and would need a rain check, but really would love to go out with you in the near future. I hope this won't discourage you for when I can accommodate you. I just need a little more time."

I started to doubt my ability to deal with a totally new situation. Maybe I should get myself back to the social scene—you know, hit the clubs for a while, but where? Suburbs or the capital city?

I decided to jump in headfirst and get back to the big leagues, so the big city it would be. I heard of a new club called the Butterfly that recently opened in one of the large hotels downtown. This was to be my objective.

Little did I know a special event was awaiting me. Something that would give my confidence and ego a healthy boost! Not knowing what might happen or who you might meet on a night out always made things incredibly exciting. I had almost forgotten how that felt!

The "Mission Impossible" Challenge

I didn't know who I might meet or run into by chance at this club; I was pleasantly surprised to run into Mike and Frank, a couple of guys I hadn't seen in awhile.

The feeling was mutual. Of course, I did get the "where have you been?" from them!

I informed them, "I've been preoccupied with the women I had in my life, and my sons had recently come to live with me."

They responded, "That's great that your sons are with you now, but we missed the little game we used to play with you."

"Oh, you mean the one where you guys pick out the woman that appears to be the hardest one to obtain and challenge me to get her," I recollected with them.

With a robust measure of enthusiasm, they replied, "Ya! We missed that little game. You were so good at it, you hardly ever failed!"

Accommodating them, I inquired, "So who do you guys have for me tonight?"

Laying down the challenge, they informed me, "Well, tonight it will be a little different. All we want you to do is get a certain woman to slow-dance with you at least once."

"Is that all?" I responded, puzzled at how easy that sounded.

"Ya, but this one just might be a 'mission impossible'!" they mysteriously implied.

"Okay, guys, you've got my attention," I proclaimed. "So where's this 'mission impossible'?"

"Jim, you see that table over there"—Frank pointed to our right—"with that very good-looking young woman in the purple dress, sitting with those two big guys?" he instructed.

I took a double take! "Hey, wait a minute, Frank, is that who I think it is?" I proclaimed.

"Well, if you're thinking Apollonia from the movie *Purple Rain*, then you're right!" they enlightened me.

"Hey, guys, you gotta be joking!" I interjected.

Their words of encouragement were, "Come on, Jim, you're the only guy in this whole club that even stands a chance!"

I took a moment to give this some thought. I decided, What the hell, go for it!

"Okay, I'll give it a shot! First, let me finish my drink, and you get someone to request the DJ to play a slow song," I said, accepting their "mission impossible" challenge.

Reconfirming the location of her table, I took a long look at her.

"Hey, guys, she really is extremely gorgeous. You think her leading man would mind?" I interjected.

"Jim, her leading man isn't here, so what he don't know won't hurt him or you," they assured me. "The guys with her are bodyguards, and a body like hers does need guarding!"

"Listen, guys, this is just one slow dance with her, right? Because I really don't believe I could get any further with her than that!" I stipulated.

"Ya, just one slow dance. If you get that much, then you are *da man*!" they agreed, giving me a vote of confidence.

Waiting for the DJ to play a requested slow song, I finished my drink; and having mustered up what little courage this required, I set out to execute this so-called mission impossible.

The first obstacle was the bodyguards. Just be cool. No sudden moves, and they shouldn't get too defensive. Slowly I walked up to her table, stopped, and slowly turned to face her. Her bodyguards stood up!

In a soft but forceful voice, she ordered them, "Boys, please, chill out and sit down! I would like to see what the gentleman wants."

"Sorry if they startled you!" she apologized and continued, "Hi, sweetie, what is it you want?"

Politely I answered, "I . . . would be honored if you would grant me the pleasure of dancing you!"

"Yes, I would love to dance with you!" she graciously accepted my invitation.

So we danced. Oh yeah, I was "da man" now!

While we danced, she informed me, "Thank you very much for having the nerve to ask me to dance. I was so bored just sitting there, watching people dancing and having fun. This is so nice, and you are too.

All I could muster was, "Thank you. You're very welcome!"

"By the way, I know you know my name, so what is yours?" she inquired.

I simply answered, "Jim."

My god, she smelled so good. It was all I could do to stay relaxed and make sure my hands were always in an appropriate place.

We finished our dance, I escorted her to her table, and the bodyguards looked relieved.

Back at the bar, my buddies were pointing out to everyone that the guy dancing with Apollonia was their friend, Jim. Returning to the bar, I got the "you are da man" reception.

One last thing to add, the icing on the cake, as it were. Standing at the bar somewhat near the front entrance/exit door, as Apollonia walked by me to leave the club, she stopped, turned to address me, sweetly saying, "Good night, Jim, and thank you once again for the dance!"

That got everyone's attention!

They teased me by quoting her, sarcastically, "Good night, Jim! Good night, Jim!"

We all had a good laugh!

For a good while after that, people would ask me, "Aren't you the guy that danced with Apollonia at the Butterfly?" But eventually, it stopped.

Rejection is the number one killer of confidence, so most men avoid situations where it could happen. Like asking a woman to dance, never mind asking them out on a date. Not that you lose it; it just kind of fades. All you've got to do is rebuild it, and when you are young, you have a lot of ways to do this. Having someone like Apollonia accept my dance invitation did it for me. That was a night of getting back my confidence. I must say, it was a very momentous night.

Rejection a.k.a. getting no for an answer is a big problem for most men, but I've tried to teach them that, from time to time, they'll get rejected—hey, even I do—so getting rejected is not the real problem. It's how many times it happens that should concern them. If it happens a lot, then they need to change their approach. It's really that simple!

Now that my confidence level was back to where it should be, I decided to continue patronizing some new clubs in the capital city and also return to some of my old favorites. Even the ones Gail and I had been to.

Subconsciously looking to run into Gail! But that would take a lot longer than I could have imagined, and time would make me more prepared for that encounter. Still, she was always somewhere in my thoughts. Try as I did, there was no way to stop them! It was always my wish to see her again. It would have to be a spontaneous meeting. I was never the type to pursue someone to the point of it appearing that I was stalking them.

I would continue my laid-back pursuit of Deidre, but now I would turn it down another notch. Not asking her to go out with me, I would portray the male friend, not a boyfriend, someone she can talk to. For women, that can be just as important as being a lover; to some, even more important. To be interested in their mind more than their body makes a large impact because most men are only interested in women for sex, and believe me, women know it!

The other thing I needed to do was to definitely spend more time with my sons. Not that I wasn't spending a lot of time with them already. I just felt they needed more of me in their lives. Also had to tend my business and keep that going. Remember, I was a one-man operation, so I did everything myself, which consumed quite a lot of my time and energy.

Early 1985

I had a strong feeling that some imperative things would be happening this year. Not so much as life changing, more like life improving. As usual, I didn't know when or what it would be.

The mysteries of life are what make it exciting! If we knew what was coming, we could prepare for it better, but where's the fun in that?

So I would now split my time up as thus: the business, my sons, and my weekend clubbing and/or dating, but not necessarily in that order. The clubbing produced quite a few one-night stands, or someone I would date once or twice with no real interest in going any further than that, either on her part or mine.

That was okay for now; I wasn't meeting anyone that made a big impression on me anyway. There were even some women who just wanted to have sex with me because I was for them a reflection of a performer of film or stage they would like to sleep with, and I would be the closest they would most likely ever get. Unfortunately, most of these women's names are lost to my memory, and some of there faces too.

What is more memorable to me is what event might have taken place at any given date, and by the way, they are far too many to go into at this time.

One more time: no brag, just fact.

And with all due respect, they didn't make a very big impact on my life anyway. It was mostly the "two ships passing in night" thing.

1985 Midsummer

What would now come to impact my life was not a woman at all. Although, it involved a woman, but not in a way anyone would have liked it to. What I'm referring to is my divorce trial; I finally had a court date: August 16, 1985.

Sweet freedom was now so close, I could taste it. I was nervous about what the outcome would or could be. To get this over and done with, I would have to agree to having been cruel and abusive to my wife as the reason for the divorce. My concern was if I agreed to these terms, would I still get to see my sons?

My lawyer assured me, "Jim, you have nothing to worry about. You're going to get to see your sons more than you could imagine, trust me."

I will not bore you with the details, but the end result was, I walked out of that courtroom with full physical custody of my sons with Mary having visiting rights, determined by the boys and their mother. I had very little, if no involvement at all in it unless things got out of hand.

Kind of strange that a judge would grant the divorce because I was cruel and abusive to my wife, yet would give me full physical custody of my sons, which goes to show you that the reasons are more or less bulls—t. They just need to fill in a reason that the law requires, meaning, the reason used is not always the real one, but lack of love or no-fault were not accepted as legitimate reasons in my state in 1985. And speaking of 1985, my lawyer informed me that I was the first man in my state to walk out of a divorce case with full physical custody of the children; a precedent had now been set for future child custody cases in my state.

All right! I had won. I was now legally free from Mary. I believed there were reasons for me to be. I had a strong feeling that my freedom was what I needed because of some events that were in my future that I could only do if I were free to pursue them. I could now get on with my life. With the autonomy to do anything I would like to, believe you me, meeting someone to marry them was the farthest thing from my mind.

I would now focus on my legal liberation to do what I wanted, when I wanted, for as long as I wanted! I would take my pleasures where I found them, and like I said before, there were lots; you should know what I mean by now. Although this time I had kept in touch with Deidre, either I would call her or she would call me, there was something about her that kept me interested, except I couldn't quite put my finger on it. I've lived long enough by now to know that there's a reason for everything, and in the fullness of time, it would make itself clear.

So somewhere in the future, there was an answer for my interest in her. Did I want to know that answer? You can bet on it! I had strong inklings that something was going on in Deidre's life, which however, at this time, she didn't want to tell me about. I surmised she was or has been going through some considerable changes, and these changes weren't anything in which I could have ever imagined.

But something was coming that would make an incredible impact in my life; it had something to do with my contact with Deidre. Knowing and feeling this, I had to do all I could to see this through to whatever end there would be. Bitter or sweet, bad or good, win or lose. I had made myself a promise to finish what I had tried to start! No matter what the results would be. For you see, I already had a significant amount of loose ends, and I didn't want to add to them.

I don't think I have mentioned this yet: I have always had an insatiable curiosity, which has gotten me into numerous tight spots.

What is it they say? "Curiosity killed the cat, but satisfaction brought him back!"

Chapter Six-Part Two

The Truth at Last

1985 Early Winter

ON A COLD winter's night, the phone rang. I answered it.
"Hello?"

"Hi, sweetie. How've you been?" Deidre's voice pronounced.

Sweetie was what she called me. Seemed like women always had a pet name for me. I never minded because it would perpetually give me an endearing feeling! Even my mother would affectionately call me lover; I believe this came from her knowing how much I loved her!

Deidre and I had not talked since before I went to court.

"How did you make out in court with your divorce?" she asked.

"We, meaning my son's and I, made out better than expected. I was given full physical custody of the boys, with their mother getting visiting rights at the discretion of the boys, so if they wanted to spend time with their mother and she was in agreement, then they did! And I would not interfere," I informed her.

"Knowing you the way I do, I'm not at all surprised, but I knew it was what you and your sons wanted to have happened. Jim, you were born to be a father, simply because it comes so natural to you. One of the reasons why what I am about to relate to you, I feel you will completely understand. First let me clear up the mystery of you and I not getting together. A short while after we met, I got pregnant by my on-again, off-again boyfriend. He told me he wanted to and would marry me, but I didn't quite believe him and my instincts turned out to be right. Now I know it seemed to you like I was just stringing you along, but the truth was you were someone I could talk to, a really good friend, someone I could trust. I feared telling you too soon, you may not have wanted to stay in contact with me anymore. And yes, when I met you, I was and still am very much attracted to you.

"The father of my child has left me to have this baby on my own. His father is going to help me a little because he's a politician and he doesn't want any kind of a scandal. So please be patient a little longer. I'm very close to my delivery date. I plan on having the baby and getting settled somewhere. And then, if you are still interested, nothing would give me more pleasure than to have you in our lives—the baby and me, that is," she explained at length.

"Well, thanks for clearing up the mystery!" I graciously replied.

The question in my mind was, *would it be worth the wait?*

I had a strange feeling that Deidre was to bring something very significant into my life.

I replied to her, saying, "Deidre, I have no immediate plans on going anywhere, and I don't see myself meeting anyone worth starting a relationship with right now or in the near future. So I guess I could wait a little longer. But please keep in mind, Deidre, that in life, there are no guarantees."

"When the time comes, Jim, and it will, and if you still have the desire to be in my life, I will do my best to make the wait worth your while," she proclaimed.

I would spend the waiting time doing what I had been doing—you know, spending time with my sons, running my business, and continuing to take my pleasures where I found them. I would play the field and reap the harvest, being a young single man; I'd suck in all the good things in life I could find! Deidre and I would still be in contact by telephone so as for me to keep track of her progress. Strange as it sounds, she would never ask me how I was spending my time waiting for her to open her life to me; she might have been apprehensive of what she might hear. Judging by the telephone number she gave me, she was living in a city bordering the next state to the south.

And if it was meant to be, then it would be. I had to wait and see, but I was never any good at waiting. Patience was not one of my strong points; my accelerated way of life never helped me with having them.

Patronizing the clubs as much as I did, women came to know things about me. Where they obtained the knowledge, I really couldn't say. I just figured if you circulate long enough, you build a reputation and that reputation tends to precede you. The word that circulated about me was that I had had a vasectomy and was

"baby safe." For whatever reason, that made women more attracted to me! So I got used a lot, but not abused, by women for their personal pleasures and found out firsthand what women go through as a one-night stand! This gave me even more respect for them than I already had.

Please don't think that I didn't have a good time pleasing them, because I really wasn't looking for anything long term anyway. Like I said before, I'd take my pleasures where I found them, and I found that giving women sexual bliss gave me satisfaction, in more ways than one!

I guess you could say I was some sort of a gigolo, but it really was all good for all parties concerned. Oh yeah, I was having a hell of a time, and no one seemed to be getting hurt.

To sum things up, I met and made love to a great deal of women at this time of my life.

I've been known to say that I've refused more women than most men have had.

One more time: No brag, just fact!

But please believe me: I always respected each and every one of them and always gave them the option to see me again if they so desired. The truth is, we all, men and women alike, have needs; and we should feel free to fulfill them.

1986

My lifestyle, I guess you could've called it promiscuous, went on for most of 1986. Had telephone contact with Deidre from time to time, but there was a hiatus in December of 1985 when she went in to have the baby. When she could get back to me, she had informed me that she had had a daughter and named her Gabrielle, and I felt and told her that it was wonderful. But the downside to this was she had lost her modeling future in the process, and she wondered what she would do for an income. She didn't really want to live on welfare or depend on a man for support. I've always told her, when she was ready to go to work, that she was an intelligent woman and would have no trouble finding something.

When we had our conversations, she would always ask how the boys were and, sometimes but not too often, asked what I had been up to. Not wanting to be disrespectful, I wouldn't mention my promiscuous lifestyle. I would simply tell her I was keeping busy with the boys, my business, and going out with the guys, which wasn't too far from the true.

She had mentioned a few times that she wanted us to get together soon and wanted to plan something that would be very special, proclaiming, "I'll think of something I believe you would really like, and we can plan on a time that would be good for both of us."

"That sounds great. I'm thinking mid-autumn before the holidays," I answered.

"That looks doable. I should have cleared up any of my loose ends by then, and so as soon as I think of something, we can discuss it, okay?" she declared.

"Sounds good!" I agreed.

1986 Mid-Autumn

A Family Ambiance

(◊"Spy in the House of Love"◊ Was (Not Was))

Deidre's midweek phone call was to inform me she had come up with an idea and wanted to run it by me. Her plan was as follows.

On the very next Saturday, I was invited to spend the day and Sunday with her and Gabrielle, who was now almost a year old, at her place about twenty-five miles south of me. This meant spending the night with Deidre. As you already know, I had anticipated this for quite a while; and with all the phone contact we had had with each other, there had been conversations about sexual likes and dislikes. She had enough information about me to accomplish a very successful seduction, if it so pleased her to do so. For this, I was slightly apprehensive about being with her, not to mention, spending the night with her.

I guess you could say she had very good intuition because she had planned this on a weekend my sons would be spending with their mother. Was it just pure coincidence?

I agreed to her plan. She then gave me the directions to her place.

Aside from packing for an overnight stay, I was set to go!

Might I add, I was very flattered by the fact that this was more than the routine first date, but whoever said I did anything routinely?

Most of my first dates lasted for more than one day. I've been known to have first dates that lasted three or four days and, more often than not, at the woman's request! I always enjoyed being in the presence of a woman who fed my ego, and fortunately, I had had many a woman like that.

Okay, enough about me. I'll now get back to my weekend with Deidre and her almost-a-year-old daughter, Gabrielle.

Embracing the Unknown

You never really know if what you are about to embrace will make your life better or worse. I like to believe you will always get a measure of both, hoping the good outweighs the bad.

For you would never know and appreciate the good if you don't experience the bad.

These were my thoughts as I drove south to my destination.

It was to be a twenty-five-minute trip to Deidre's place. I had left my place about eight thirty in the morning, to get there around nine or so.

Deidre had informed me that they usually have breakfast between nine and ten on a Saturday morning, so if I would like to have breakfast with them, I should arrive accordingly. I did like the idea of having breakfast with them, and I believe I had planned it just about right.

I got to the center of her town, found a payphone to call her to let her know I was close by, and asked if she wanted me to pick up anything at the store she might need.

She informed me, "You are so sweet. I don't have any beer, wine, or soda in the house right now, so you can get whatever you would desire to drink. And if you are going to watch the game on Sunday, you might want to get some snacks that you like. Oh ya, I could use a half gallon of low-fat milk. That should do it. And thanks, you are so considerate. By the way, do you like waffles?"

"Yes, I like waffles!" I replied.

"That's great, because that's what we're having this morning, so we should see you here in about ten minutes." she proclaimed.

"That sounds just about right. I'm really looking forward to meeting Gabrielle!" I told her.

"And I believe she's looking forward to meeting you!" Deidre announced.

"I'll see you two soon," I declared and hung up the phone.

Finally arriving at her condo complex, I just had to find the one that was hers. Finding her unit number, I parked my car in her visitors' spot. Grabbed what I had picked up from the store and my overnight bag, took a deep breath, and made my way to her door. No matter how many times I do things like this, the first time always makes me a little nervous. For not only was I partaking in something I had waited quite awhile to happen, I was also meeting Gabrielle, a little girl. I only knew about raising boys. Spending time with a little girl would be something new, and we all know new can be a little scary.

I had hoped Gabrielle would like me and feel comfortable with me.

Spending Time with Angels

I stood at her front door for a moment of reflection and then put my finger on the bell and pressed. It rang. I could hear Deidre say,

"I'm coming, Jim."

That statement always has a double meaning to me, I thought to myself, just trying to lighten myself up. The door opened. To my pleasant surprise, Deidre had not lost too much of her model's figure, and her face had a sweet glow to it, a motherly one I would say. A few added pounds, but in all the right places, she still looked very desirable.

"Hi, sweetie, please come in. I hope you're hungry. Give me the food you bought. You can put your bag down there. I'll take it upstairs to my bedroom later," she declared.

I made my way to the table and sat down. Said hello to Gabrielle, and she smiled at me. That was a good sign. It was the smile of an angel. She was as beautiful as a child her age could be. Deidre came to the table with some delicious looking waffles and, while filling my plate, introduced me to her daughter.

"Gaby, this is Mommy's friend, Jim. He is going to be visiting with us for a few days!"

Gaby, short for *Gabrielle,* smiled at me again and, with her outstretched hand, offered me a piece of waffle from her plate saying something that sounded like "Waffa?"

Deidre informed me, "She really likes you, Jim. She only offers her food to people she likes. This is a good thing. After breakfast, I have some housework to do. I really have to straighten up my bedroom, so you and Gaby can spend some time together. That sound good, Jim and Gaby?"

"Sounds great," I replied.

Gaby just smiled and offered me another piece of her waffa, as she called it.

I leaned to her so she could put in my mouth. Having done this, she laughed and said something else I didn't quite understand.

With breakfast finished, Deidre cleaned up the table and Gaby.

I made my way to the couch and put on the television. Deidre brought Gaby over and put her on the floor in front of me with some of her toys and asked if I wanted another cup of coffee, and in saying yes to her, she got it for me. I split my time between watching television and attending to Gaby. I made her laugh a few times. Deidre heard her and delightfully called out from upstairs,

"What's going on down there?"

"Nutten', honey!" I mischievously answered her.

"You two better play nice!" Deidre playfully proclaimed.

"Yes, Mom!" I jokingly answered.

The day seemed to slip away. It had begun to get dark, and Gaby was now starting to fall asleep on the floor. Deidre took notice of this and said to me, "Wow! You really got her tired. She's just about ready for bed. I'll take her up to her room. While I'm up there, I'll change into something more comfortable. Jim, you could put on some music and open the wine. That would be nice, if that's okay with you? And I'll be right down."

"Ya, that sounds good to me!" I replied.

The moment of truth approaches! No matter how many times I experience this, it never seems to get old or easier.

For me, there always seems to be an aura of electricity in the air. In one or two of our conversations, we had talked about an evening like this, and she relayed what she would like to see happen. I had told her if certain things I requested of her were fulfilled, I would be at her service.

Deidre had informed me she liked to wear satin and lace nightgowns that were formfitting, and no panties. I told her, "That works for me!"

I wanted to have the wine poured just before she came down, so I softly called up to her to let me know when she would be coming down. She agreed. About five minutes later, I heard her say softly,

"Jim, I'm coming!"

There's that phrase again! A premeditated statement?

Deidre descended the stairs looking like dream in white satin and lace.

I proclaimed softy and slightly breathless, "God, help me!"

She replied seductively, "Not a chance in hell!"

Our intimate encounter was one for the history books. An event happened that most people hope for, but very seldom obtain.

After about an hour of foreplay on the couch, we made our way upstairs where we became one; and for the first and unfortunately the last time, we achieved simultaneous bliss! I do believe you know what I mean.

As much as we tried to achieve it again, we couldn't.

It really was amazing. All I had ever heard it was! I could now say the wait was well worth it, but not just for the sex.

The next day, Sunday, was a perfect family day. I watched the game while keeping an eye on Gaby, with Deidre cooking dinner and coming to see from time to time how the game was going.

Deidre informed me she would be moving soon. Gaby's grandfather needed to sell the condo, for you see, the condo was to be Deidre and his son's marital home. This meant Deidre would have to find a place to go, so it might be awhile before we'd see each other again. I had a feeling she was hoping that I would offer her and Gaby to come and live with me and the boys, but I didn't have the room. I did tell her I would if I could; she understood and was grateful for the thought.

It became time for me to go. A sad farewell but a happy thought that we would all see each other soon. Deidre told me that once she got settled in a new place, she'd call and we'd do this again.

I agreed, gave them both a kiss, reminded Deidre to call me as soon as she had a place to live.

I really felt bad that I couldn't take them in. Knowing what I know now, and you will too soon, I now see that if I could have, the relationship between Deidre and I would have gone much better.

I drove back home with my mind beset with all kinds of *coulda'*, *shoulda'*, *woulda'*. Our time together could not have gone more perfect; and when you experience what seems like perfection, you sure would like to stay that way, at least for a while.

I did like Deidre a lot and, with time, would probably have come to love her and could also experience what it would be like to have a daughter that I couldn't have on my own. Only the future would tell, and not knowing what it would hold for us, there would be no way of preparing for it. Because most of the time in life, you just hold on as tight as you can and go for the ride.

I truly believe we are only in control of 50 percent of our lives. The other 50 percent is up to fate, time and place, or luck.

End of Chapter Six

Chapter Seven-Part One

When It Rains, It Pours!

Early 1987

I HAD NO IDEA when I would hear from Deidre. The phone number she had given me became useless; it had been disconnected not long after I spent the weekend with her and Gabrielle. So I would have to wait for her to contact me. So once again, I needed to occupy my time. The only thing to do was go back to the social scene.

The social scene had become slightly more standoffish; the spreading of the AIDS virus would account for this. It had become more and more dangerous to be too promiscuous. Just to remind you, up until AIDS, social diseases weren't so deadly and had a somewhat common cure. Penicillin generally worked on most of them, but this treatment had no effect against AIDS. As a result, everybody was being extra careful about who they had sex with. So it goes without saying that my licentious lifestyle would have to change because now, one mistake would kill me! One thing that hadn't changed was that cocaine was still being widely and frequently used by the populace!

This made socializing somewhat less fun; women would now keep a partner that they knew was not infected with AIDS or look for someone that they knew wasn't infected. Easier said than done. Only a blood test could detect if a person was infected with AIDS, and they weren't 100 percent accurate.

However, the social scene did continue with some noticeable changes! People weren't so ready, willing, and able to get physical right away, men and women alike.

Therefore, I made some alterations by slowing it down, like trying to take the time to get to know a woman I had just met before getting physically intimate with her. Unless the situation dictated differently. There still were those rare times when we'd cast our fate to the wind and just go for it!

Note: It was not a common practice of mine to use condoms. I had tried them once, awhile ago, and didn't like them. They hindered my performance.

Fortunately, I didn't have to tolerate this for too long, for you see, about mid-January, I heard from Deidre. She gave me some semigood news. She had to find an income very quickly and having been in the modeling business, when modeling got slow, she'd do some work as an escort. Sex was not included; a customer would have to pay extra for that. She had left Gabrielle with her mother, Rita, and was now residing at a house in a northern suburb where an escort service was being run from. Deidre, knowing I felt somewhat uneasy about this, informed me this was only a temporary situation until she could find something else; but for the time being, she would do this.

Deidre also enlightened me that any and all physical contact of any kind with a customer had to be done using a condom, no exceptions, except for me, if I so desired to be with her! But she would understand if I now was disinterested in being in her life. The strange thing was, in a weird way, this made me even more attracted to her. I always found that a diminutive element of danger proved to make things slightly more exciting!

So for reasons of my own, I stayed in contact with her. One of the reasons was that I was very fond of Gaby, strictly in a fatherly way. After all, I was the best chance she had of having a father figure in her life. My first objective was to find out where Deidre's mother lived and go introduce myself to her to get into Gaby's life and give her a father figure that all children should have. I had no doubt that I could accomplish this. I enjoyed being with someone I looked at as a daughter, seeing I was not able to ever have one of my own. I wanted to be that father figure that Gaby would need, especially with the noticeable absence of her mother in her life.

If I could start spending time with Gaby, and Deidre knew this, it could inspire her to get out of the business she was in. You see, Rita had taken legal custody of Gaby and stopped Deidre from having any contact with her. Because not only was Deidre working as an escort, her cocaine use was getting to be habitual.

I found out where Rita lived and went to meet her and introduce myself. Surprisingly, Rita knew who I was. Deidre had told her all about me and that Gaby was very fond and comfortable with me and that I could be trusted. That was made obvious to her because when Gaby saw me, she ran to me, said my name, and gave me a big hug. This was a reunion that I hoped would be the beginning of a father-daughter relationship with Gaby and me!

Rita agreed to let me spend time with Gaby on a Saturday or Sunday for about two or three hours, to start with. I totally understood that I would have to prove that I could be trusted; she was more concerned that I might allow Deidre to have contact with Gaby while in my care. Rita was totally against that for the time being. Knowing how strongly she felt about this, I would abide by her wishes. This was something that would help me win her trust of me. Gaby had not learned to lie yet, so everything we did together, she would tell her grammy; so doing anything out of line was totally out of the question!

Rita had now come to feel strongly that I could be trusted because around the house, Gaby was referring to me as Daddy, so much so that she asked me to be Gaby's godfather. For you see, Gaby had not been baptized yet, and it needed to be done; I accepted gracefully and replied, "I'd be honored."

"Good. I'll get started on making the arrangements," Rita replied.

This was the opportunity to possibly motivate Deidre, because if she wanted to have contact with her daughter, she would have to straighten out her act, such as getting a legitimate job and refraining from the cocaine use.

The time I would spend with Gaby made me especially happy. Ever since I was a young boy, when I was feeling forlorn, I would sit off in the distances of a playground and watch the children at play with each other. This gave me solace—to see them enjoying the simple things in life; they were on a natural high. They reminded me to appreciate those simple things that I had forgotten or was taking for granted. So being around children always made me feel better. That was probably why I found it very undemanding to be a parent. I had no idea the very important role Gaby would be playing in my life in the near future.

Deidre, now knowing that I was spending time with her daughter and was to be her godfather, realized that I could be the instrument in her having contact with her daughter, but only if she made some changes in her lifestyle. She knew I was the one to help bridge the gap among her, her mother, and her daughter, in many ways.

One of the reasons Deidre worked as an escort, besides the money, was because it gave her a place to live. This became the center of a conversation that went like so:

"Jim, if I had a place to live and someone in my life to share mutual affections with, it would give me the support I would need to make the changes to help me get my daughter back in my life," she proclaimed.

Okay, I'm beginning to get the feeling that I've painted myself onto a corner.

"Deidre, I do want to help you, but having you come to live with me might not work out!" I stated.

"If you would allow me this, I would immediately change my occupation and get off the cocaine too. I promise I would!" she claimed.

"Give me a few days to think about it, and I'll let you know," I insisted.

Well, I took the next few days and weighed out the pros and cons of the situation. I will spare you the details.

I decided to give Deidre a chance to get herself straight because I was the only one that could do this for her at this time. I informed my sons of my decision; they didn't seem to mind. They were now old enough to realize that when Dad had a woman in his life, he was a little more accommodating about everything.

I would call her on Friday afternoon and tell her and see if she could make the move on Saturday. Of course, I would help her do this. It really wouldn't be that difficult. All she had was her clothes.

She was very happy to hear of my decision, but informed me that she would need about a week to clear up her scheduled obligations.

And in the meantime, she would contact some temp work offices and apply for work. That worked better than I figured because I had forgotten that I needed some time to make room for her and her clothes. I informed Rita of the situation, and she declared that if Deidre could get herself straightened out, she would consider letting her see Gaby under my supervision. I would have to be there, I agreed with her.

With anticipation Deidre informed me that on the very next Saturday, she would be ready to make the move. That move went rather smoothly. Like I said before, all she had was her clothes. She spent most of the day putting her clothes away. Deidre informed me that she wanted to make a nice dinner for me and the boys and sent me, with a list, to the supermarket to get what she needed, which got me and the boys out of her way.

I had almost had forgotten how domestic she could be and a good cook too, remembering that Sunday dinner she had made when I was with her and Gaby awhile back for a couple of days.

It wasn't long before she had gotten some temp work in the next town to the south, which she could get to in the morning using public transportation; I was able to pick her up when her workday ended. And yes, she did stop using cocaine; I knew this because other than the time she spent at work, she was with me. Besides, she wasn't making the amount of money to support that type of habit.

1987 Midspring

Deidre was holding up to her promise, so I felt it was time to see if Rita would allow her to see Gaby. With a little reluctance, she agreed, but only if I was going to be with them.

Deidre had not seen her daughter in a while and was afraid that Gaby wouldn't recognize her; I assured her that the mother-and-child bond was one of strongest on earth and that a child could not forget their mother. On the appointed Saturday, I went to pick up Gaby and bring her to my house where Deidre nervously waited, wondering how it would go. Needless to say, it went precisely the way I told Deidre it would. When Gaby saw Deidre, she called out, "Mommy!" and ran to her! The smile on Deidre's face could not have been any bigger or brighter. With Gaby in her arms, she turned to me, kissed me, and said, "Thank you for this, Jim!"

Things were going rather good. Everyone seemed happy with the way things were; even Rita was getting comfortable with Gaby spending time with Deidre, so much so that she would now allow Gaby to spend the weekends with us. I felt Deidre was getting very comfortable with us being kind of a family and had thoughts of us getting married.

She had talked about us being together that way, but I wasn't sure enough of my feelings to even consider it at this time. She had told me on several occasions that she had strong feeling for me and so did her daughter. I must admit I wasn't too comfortable with the trappings of marriage.

The conditions of marriage were not something I really wanted to get back into without being as sure as I could possibly be that I was absolutely ready.

(◊ "I Just Can't Stop Loving You" ◊ Michael Jackson)

My parents had now moved into the second floor of the house.

Needless to say, having my father living in the house made me very uncomfortable.

Jim, my older son, had now obtained driver's licenses—one for a car and one for a motorcycle. The café racer style motorcycle was the most popular of that time; a lot of his friends were buying them. This meant he also wanted one. He had talked to a dealer and could get the one he wanted, but he would need a cosigner for the loan.

Of course, he came to me first. I was not happy that he wanted a motorcycle, so I asked if he would wait until he was a little older to do this. I felt seventeen was too young, and nineteen would be better because usually, the older you are, the more responsible you were, which meant to me that he'd be more cautious.

He refused to wait, so I refused to be his cosigner. In failing to get me to do this for him, he next went to his mother, who agreed to sign and also bought him a helmet. I felt strongly that this kind of encouragement was an opening for a disaster just waiting to happen.

Just to recap, Deidre and I were getting along fairly well. Gaby was now staying at my house for the weekends. We were now playing at being a family, and Deidre was starting to get ideas of her own about us becoming just that.

But something was about to happen that would truly test the depth of our relationship.

1987 Father's Day Misfortune

I was looking forward to a pleasant fun-filled summer, but unfortunately, this was not to be.

Gaby had not stayed over on this particular Saturday because Rita had plans that included her for Sunday, so Deidre and I were having a Father's Day lie-in, a little extra be together time.

We had just finished enjoying extra time together when the phone rang. Answering it, I heard a male stranger's voice ask, somewhat frantically, "Hello, is this Jim Sr.?"

"Yes it is, who are you?" I answered.

"Who I am is not important. Your son Jim has been in a motor vehicle accident!" he informed me.

"O my god! Where and when?" I anxiously inquired.

He then informed me of the time and place.

I hung up the phone, immediately started dressing, informing Deidre of what had happened while I finished.

I rushed to the scene of the accident to find my son lying on the grass to the far side of the intersection where the accident happened.

I ran to his aid; there wasn't much I could do for him. The police on the scene had informed me that an ambulance was on the way. I leaned over him and saw he was awake and he had removed his helmet; he looked up at me with tear-filled eyes and said, "Dad, I'm sorry!"

A chill went up my spine. I will never forget those words. He was in a great deal of pain, and his left leg was bleeding badly. The paramedics arrived and carefully picked him up and rushed him off to the nearest hospital.

Jim requested that I stay and wait for the tow truck for his bike, which looked to me to be totaled. So I instructed the tow truck diver to take it to my house and to put in the garage; he would follow me to the house.

I picked up Jim's helmet, which was cracked; I thought, *Better the helmet than his head*, got in my car, and headed for home with the tow truck carrying the bike following me.

Luckily, my mother was not home when I got to the house, because if she saw the bike, she would have freaked. I went in the house to tell Deidre what had happened and that I needed to get back to the hospital where they had taken my son Jim, knowing they really couldn't do much for him until I got there because he was only seventeen. She requested to go with me; I agreed. We arrived at the hospital to find that they had contained the bleeding, given him something for the pain, and took a primary X-ray to find that the bone in his left leg was not broken, but splintered! I then told the doctor I needed to make a phone call; it was to the doctor who had replaced my mother's hip. Telling him the situation, he demandingly instructed me, "Do not leave him there! Have him transported to the general hospital in the capital city, and I will meet you there."

When we got there, the doctor took over the situation and got Jim in for more X-rays. After about an hour or so, he came in to where Deidre and I were waiting to see him. He informed me that it was a very bad injury, which would take some time to repair and then heal. We needed to get him into the OR as quickly as possible. I had to sign all the paperwork myself because in my attempts to contact his mother, she was nowhere to be found. I finally got in touch with her; and soon after, she showed up, demanding to see Jim, but he had already gone into the OR. It was to be a nine-hour operation. After about three hours or so, a doctor from the team that was aiding in the operation came to inform me and Deidre, whom he addressed as my son's mother a.k.a. my wife. From the other side of the room, my ex-wife, Mary, proclaimed harshly,

"Excuse me, Doctor. I'm the boy's mother!"

Well, he claimed, then turning in his chair to address all of us, that the procedure was going well so far, and after the operation, he would be spending a lot of time in the hospital for recovery and to safeguard against any infection. He might need some physical therapy, but for now, all that could be done was being done. Then he suggested that we all go home to eat and try to get some rest; they would call me when he was in recovery.

As they had said, he went into recovery, and the call I received was very good news. They had managed to save his leg, which I was very grateful and relieved to learn about. But he would be spending a lot of time in the hospital. It turned out to be a nine-week stay. Of course, we had gotten a lawyer to get the financial things taken care of, which were achieved.

During the first week or so of Jim's stay in the hospital, Deidre informed me that she wasn't up to dealing with all this, what she referred to as an interruption in her life, and decided to move out. I didn't oppose her on this issue for I had too much to deal with to take on any more. She told me she would go stay with a girlfriend, so she packed up and left. At that moment, I felt she had abandoned me in a time of great need and to myself decided I had no desire to sustain any future relationship with her, although I still wished to continue to have Gaby in my life, and I did.

Chapter Seven-Part Two

More Heavy Weather!

1987 Early Summer

I, ONCE AGAIN free to do what I wanted, went back to the club scene. I would visit my son every night. On the weekends, I would stay until he fell asleep and then go out for the night. Trying to get my mind off all that had happened, socializing helped a bit, and spending time with Gaby helped even more.

One night, while at the hospital, it came to me that I should let DeeDee know what had happened to Jim. The only phone number I had for her was Loretta's, her mother's, so I went to a hospital payphone and made the call.

"Hello, Loretta, this is Jim. Is DeeDee there?" I inquired.

"Hi Jim, I assume you have not heard what has happened."

I had a really bad feeling in the pit of my stomach.

"What is it you wanted to talk to DeeDee about?" Loretta asked.

"Well, I wanted to tell her that my son Jim has been in a motor vehicle accident and that he's in the hospital recovering and is going to be okay," I explained.

"I'm sorry to hear that, Jim. What hospital is he in?" she asked.

I figured she was asking in case DeeDee wanted to visit him.

"He's in the general hospital in the capital city on the seventh floor of the south building."

"Sorry to have to tell you this, but DeeDee is also there, on the ninth floor in the same building. About a week ago, she suffered a brain aneurysm," she informed me.

"I'm so sorry to hear this. Is she okay?" I inquired.

"Jim, why not go see for yourself," she suggested.

"Thank you, Loretta. I will," I replied.

I said good-bye, hung up the phone. I looked at my watch to see that it was almost ten thirty at night. Normal visiting hours ended at ten o'clock. So I would have to come up with a way to get in to see her. I told Jim I'd be back in a while, not wanting to tell him what I had just leaned until I saw how DeeDee was, then headed to the elevators to go up to the ninth floor.

On the way up, I was trying to figure a way I might get in to see her. I thought to grab a doctor's coat. No, too extreme. I came up with something I featured might work. It was deceitful, but at times like these, it was the only way. Approaching the nurse's station, I inquired about Maureen a.k.a. DeeDee. They informed me that visiting hours were over.

I appealed to them by saying, "Thank you, ladies. I understand that."

I thought, *Trying to sound desperate might help.*

"But you see, I'm Maureen's uncle, Jim. And just this morning, I found out what had happened to her, flew in from the coast on the first flight I could get, and would be obliged if you would let me visit with her for just a few minutes."

One of the nurses felt badly about my plight and suggested she would see if Maureen was awake and ask if she would like to see her uncle Jim. She returned a moment later to say, "Okay, she'll see you but, please, only for a few minutes. She's in private room 221 at the end of the corridor on the left."

"Thank you so much. You're very kind," I appreciatively answered.

Walking down the corridor, I had no idea what to expect. This was a young woman I had felt a great deal of emotion for, and still did somewhat. After all, I was her first lover and had been intimate with her countless times.

I tensely approached the door to her room, stepped inside a few feet, and softly addressed her, "DeeDee?"

With slurred speech, she answered me, "Ji-Jimm!"

The room was dark, but I could still tell by her speech and her physical appearance she was profoundly affected by what had happened to her. As best as she could, she told me what had transpired. This was once what I conceived as a very beautiful young woman; she was not so much anymore. Not having a lot of time, I explained to her what had happened to my son, Jim; she was pleased to know that he would be okay. I gave her a kiss on her cheek and asked where she'd be staying when she left the hospital. She told me as best as she could, "I wi-will be-be a-at my-my mo-mu-theer's ha-houssee."

I just about understood her and on my exit replied, "Well then, I'll be in touch!"

Made my way back to the elevators, passing the nurse's station, thanking them once again. Got back to Jim's room. He was still awake, so I told him about DeeDee. He felt badly about her situation. He was getting very tried, so I said good night and left until the following night.

During my drive home, numerous thoughts about all that had occurred in the last several days felled my head. My brain was a whirlwind of assessments; things had transpired that affected other things, like the ripples from a stone dropped in water. I was too tired to think straight so I'd leave all this for when I wasn't feeling so overwhelmed.

The next day was Friday; I wasn't doing deliveries on Fridays, so I would use the day to catch up on any business paperwork. My head would have to be clear to do this work, which meant it was a good time to be lucid.

Okay, with the paperwork done, I could now collect my thoughts.

First, my older son, Jim, was in the hospital recuperating. Thank God he hadn't lost his leg. By not panicking and keeping my wits, I was able to think straight and get the right doctor and hospital for him.

Second, Deidre had left me to go do God knows what! I would now have to tell Rita. I was pretty sure she would recant Deidre's permission to see Gaby. I would have to explain this to Gaby as best as I could. I'd do it over ice cream; it always made things go easier!

Third, DeeDee was in an awful state. With her having an aneurysm, she would lose a lot of her independence. The guy she was seeing eventually would leave her. The greatest need was for her to have a friend she could trust. I guess she was looking at me to fill that spot, and a little more I assumed.

And last but surely not least, I had my younger son, Vincent, who also needed my attention; and I had my business to run. I feel tired just remembering all that was going on in my life at that time. I believe one more straw would have broken me.

How could I maintain any kind of romantic relationship with someone I might meet while out socializing? Oh I would, but it just couldn't be too intense. So it would be back to the one-night stands. With all due respect, barmaids and waitresses were always good for this, and offering them a foot massage after they were done with their night's work would always win them over!

Life was getting to be very hectic once again, everything happening at once—the ongoing effect of my accelerated life.

Someday I would have to find a way to slow it down or I was pretty sure a way would find me. Well, so much for a fun-filled summer.

1987 Late Summer

It was getting close to the time for Jim to be coming home. He would be leaving the hospital, not with a cast on his leg, for you see, he had metal rods inserted through his leg to hold the bones together and in place. Not a pretty sight. His open wounds would need to be looked after and kept clean. He also needed help getting something to eat and doing all the other things we do without really thinking about them until we can't do them for ourselves. Arrangements would need to be made for his tending to. I couldn't be home all the time because I had my business to run during the day; and my younger son, Vincent, was helping me out, so he wouldn't be home either. There was some talk about the boy's mother coming over to attend to Jim, or a visiting nurse. I agreed to the visiting nurse; I was not agreeable to his mother being around my place, especially when I wasn't there. So it would be a visiting nurse and my mom helping out as much as she could, for she lived right upstairs.

She was the best candidate and she wanted to! So when the nurse wasn't there, she could be, at least until I got home. And as I have said before, I started my day early, so I got home early; so that part of the situation seemed to be working well.

I had now talked to Rita about the way things had changed, and as I expected, she recanted Deidre's visiting rights. She didn't feel that bad about it because Gaby had me and I was sure to make the time to spend with my godchild. There was another thing I was starting to be concerned about. I noticed Rita's health was starting to fail her, granted she wasn't getting any younger, so how much longer would she be able to be Gaby's guardian? Gaby was almost three and getting to be a little hard for Rita to handle. Rita was also in the process of moving, which she felt would make it harder for Deidre to know where she and Gaby were living.

And then there was DeeDee. I would call her mother's house periodically to find out if she had left the hospital and was living there yet. Eventually, DeeDee's mom, Loretta, told me that she was; and then I got to talk to her, which was not an easy thing to do; her speech was still quite slurred.

I would have to ask her to talk slowly so that I could understand what she was saying. This was the first uncomfortable thing I would have to do; in the days that followed, there would be more.

I knew the whole situation with DeeDee would be difficult for me. I'm sorry, but as shallow as it sounds, a person's physical appearance was the first thing that attracted me to them; and knowing how much it had mattered to me that DeeDee was a very beautiful young woman made it a great deal harder. Her facial deformity took away a lot of her physical appeal for me, and her erratic physical movements made me very uncomfortable. I would visit with her to keep her company and help her pass the time, doing things for her that she had difficulty with, such as getting food and drink. Her mother and family liked this because it meant they had less to do for her.

I was now dividing my time between DeeDee, Gaby, my sons, and my business; there was barely any time for myself. Plans were in the works for getting DeeDee back to where she was living when she had the aneurysm; her mother had kept up the rent so DeeDee could go back there if she so wished when she was able. With a visiting living assistant and a motorized wheelchair, she felt she would be able to live on her own.

DeeDee was now living back in her apartment and would call me to ask me to come over to have lunch with her quite a bit.

1987 Mid-Autumn

My life now consisted of caring for my son, Jim; spending time with Gaby—I had not heard from Deidre in a while; spending time with DeeDee; and running my business with the help of my son Vincent, unless he had school. DeeDee had designs on getting me to be back in her life. As I said before, I was very uncomfortable with the condition she was in; she didn't really look or sound like the girl I knew and was once in love with.

One Sunday, she requested I come over and make dinner with her and stay the night. I reluctantly accepted her invitation, but because Monday was a workday, I wore my work clothes and slept on top of the bed blankets with my clothes on to display no interest in engaging in intimate contact with her. Needless to say, it was a very awkward situation. I didn't sleep much, and from that point on, I had less and less contact with her. I was feeling very bad about things with DeeDee. I had rejected her; and although I never told her, it was because of the way she looked, sounded, and moved.

I started to make excuses not to spend time with her; the one that ended our somewhat difficult situation was that I told her I had met someone and was very interested in having a relationship with her.

The holidays were quickly approaching, and I really wanted Gaby to have the best Christmas she could. I suggested to Rita that Gaby and I go get a Christmas tree. Rita agreed, saying, "Jim, that would be wonderful because I haven't been able to afford one in a while, but I don't have any decorations for a tree."

"No problem, Rita. I will give you mine because I don't use them anymore, and I'll buy some lights too. Not to worry, I'll take care of everything. This will be the best Christmas Gaby could ever have!" I proclaimed.

"That would be extremely nice of you, Jim! Thank you so much," Rita answered appreciatively.

Gaby and I went out to find the best Christmas tree we could, which I gladly paid for; after all, a child's happiness is priceless. At the Christmas tree lot, Gaby and I browsed for a tree; I found the one I felt was the most perfect one there. I called to Gaby, "Gaby, I think I found the one!"

Gaby came to where I was and so did the lot attendant, who asked Gaby, "So what do you think? Your daddy likes this one, do you?"

I looked at her, and she nodded yes. I told the attendant, "We'll take this one."

Back in the car, with the tree in the trunk, we sat for a minute to let the car warm up; I turned to Gaby and gently said, "The man at the tree lot thought I was your father. Are you okay with that happening?"

She looked up at me and said, "That's okay with me. I wish you really were."

Christmas morning, I arrived early to present Gaby with all the gifts I had got for her; her excitement was uncontainable! Needless to say, she had the best Christmas she'd had to date. I was so happy to be so instrumental in attaining this for her.

The day after was rather quiet, until the calm atmosphere was broken by the phone ringing. I answered it curiously, softly saying,

"Hello?"

"Hi, sweetie, how've you been?" Deidre pronounced.

End of Chapter Seven

Chapter Eight-Part One

Stark Realities

Deidre, Gabrielle, and Me

Late 1988

I REALLY WAS quite stunned that it was Deidre who was calling me on the phone. Then again, with me having contact with her mother and daughter, it was only matter of time before she would contact me. I took a moment to promptly collect my thoughts; I wanted to tell her where to go and not to call me again. On second thought, if Deidre was to get custody of Gaby in the future, it would probably jeopardize my seeing her. I had to be tactful and handle this situation with poise and finesse.

I started off cordially and upbeat with "Hi, Deidre. I'm okay, now that things have returned to as close to normal as possible, for the time being."

"Jim, that's good to hear, and how is your son Jim doing?" she stated and asked.

"As good as he can be for now," I answered.

"What does that mean? Isn't he home yet?" she inquired.

"Oh yes, he's home, but being on crutches, he can't do much for himself, so we have a visiting nurse come in. And my mother is helping out also. After some therapy, he'll be walking on his own again," I explained.

"I take it you're still spending time with my daughter?" she inquired.

"Yes, I am and happy to say that we have some good times together like real fathers and daughters do!" I explained.

"Does she ask about me?" she asked.

"Not to me. Maybe she asks your mother, Rita," I clarified.

"I'm sincerely sorry for leaving you the way I did. Can you ever forgive me?" she pleaded.

"It's taken you a very long time to fess up to it. It's been what, about six months?" I criticized.

"Well, you see, I had to get myself set up in a business of my own, a place and some girls . . . I mean, employees," she declared, trying to defend the time lapse.

"Oh, and what kind of business might that be? I'm almost afraid to ask," I reluctantly replied, not really caring to hear her answer.

"Well, if you really want to know, I decided to open and operate my own escort service. I would be running it, not actually doing any escorting myself, just like the woman I had worked for," she explained.

I would guess she thought that if she wasn't actually working as an escort and only running the business, it would be more acceptable to Rita and me.

"So where are you doing this?" I reluctantly asked.

"Actually, I'm not to far from you. I'm in the next city just south of you, in a high-rise apartment building. I got a two-bedroom apartment so the trolls a.k.a. clients, as she referred to them, could come here or we could go to them. Right now I have two girls working, and I plan to get more. So why don't you come and see for yourself? I really would like to see you," she explained.

Ya, I bet she would!

"That's okay, Deidre, I believe you. Maybe some other time," I sternly answered.

"Okay. So, sweetie, what are you doing for New Year's Eve?" she boldly asked.

"I usually don't go out for New Year's Eve," I proclaimed.

"Well, I think we should get together. Whata' ya say?" she invitingly requested.

"Thank you, Deidre, but I will have to decline," I politely refused.

"Why? Are you seeing someone and spending it with them?" she sharply inquired.

"Oh no, that's not it at all!" I reluctantly answered.

"Okay then, if you change your mind, here's my number. You can call me," she insistently stated. "By the way, how are my mother and daughter?"

I didn't want to tell her that Rita's health was failing, so I just answered her with "They're doing fine. I made sure Gaby had a really good Christmas."

"I believe you would because I know how you are," she confessed.

"Well, Deidre, I really need to get off the phone. I have some of my business paperwork to take care of. Okay then, you take care of yourself!" was my exiting statement.

"You really are a sweetheart, and I truly do care about you. Please don't be a stranger. Ciao!" she replied.

We then hung up *simultaneously*!

I was now feeling a little gloomy, to think that Deidre might get custody of Gaby shortly. I wasn't too sure what she would do about me spending time with her. She just might try to use Gaby as leverage to get things the way she wanted them to be.

As quickly as I could, I dispelled any more thoughts about it; I needed to get on with my life. This weekend being New Year's Eve, I would lay low.

Early 1989

In this New Year, I would regenerate myself and go out to see what new adventures awaited me. After all, that's what makes life exciting and worth living, for me. I had bought myself a couple of new suits and was looking forward to wearing them out to the clubs and seeing what kind of reaction I would get. Quite a few times, the ladies would break the ice with me by commenting on how much they liked my attire.

I was quite the sucker for a compliment. With me, flattery went a long way; it was one of my grand ego builders. And being given a compliment, I was quick to return one, especially if I liked who had given it to me.

It was a brand-new year, and I was feeling really good about it. With every day, my son Jim would be getting stronger. He talked about getting a car when he was well enough; not another bike, thank God!

I was not seeing DeeDee at all; she had moved about twenty miles south of the capital city. We might talk on the phone once in a while, but that would be all the contact we had. I always looked forward to spending time with Gaby on the weekends! For me, it's rather important to have something to look forward to; I think most people feel that way.

Okay, it was now time to hit some clubs and have some fun with the ladies, and I did. It didn't take me much to get back into the swing of things. I really needed this year to be a good one!

Deidre would call me on the phone from time to time to see what I had been up to. She would ask me to get together with her. I knew sooner or later I would have to get cozy with her to stay on her good side. One Sunday phone call was made to me when she was feeling sick. She claimed she was to sick to cook herself dinner, so I figured with her being sick. It might be a safe bet to visit with her, thinking she wouldn't have designs on getting or wanting any physical contact with me, because I wasn't really interested in rekindling the emotional relationship we once had.

So I accepted her invite and offered to make dinner for both of us, for you see, I was a pretty good cook. Asking her what she would like to eat for dinner, she requested spaghetti and meatballs. That was great; I was really good at Italian food. You can credit my mom for that. I had spent a lot of time in the kitchen with my mom when I was a young boy and, in doing so, learned how to cook, mostly Italian.

Deidre gave me the directions to where she was, and I made my way there. It was a pleasant enough day; we ate and talked, and as I had hoped, there wasn't any physical contact. My intention was to maintain a respectful association with her for the sake of my seeing Gaby. I had no problem relating my social activities to her, and some of them were very obscure, like receiving a wrong-number phone call early one evening that turned into a date and brief relationship or a one-night stand with a barmaid that lasted for two days. Deidre always knew I was relatively a player. She had asked if we could go out for drinks and dancing some night in the near future. Taking the female approach, I answered, "Maybe, we'll see."

She reminded me that she was only running the escort business for the money and wouldn't be in it for any longer than she need to.

Slaying the Dragon

I knew what she was getting at, and I wasn't at all comfortable with it. I well admit—*but only to you, dear reader*—I did have an affection and a fondness toward Deidre, but not strong enough to slay the dragon.

"Slaying the dragon?" you might ask, "What does that mean?"

Well, in days of old, when knights were bold, they would prove their love of a maiden by slaying the dragon that was threatening her life and village; but now that all the dragons have been slain, what it means now to a man is to commit to marriage, the dragon being a man's state of being single and free. At least, that is how I relate to it, and most of my gender would agree.

It's not that we men don't want to commit; it's just that it's such a risk for us because when a marriage fails—as they often do, for one reason or another—we're usually the ones that come out of it with the major losses.

I was one of the few-and-far-between very lucky ones to come out of my marriage as well as I did!

Oh well, Deidre aside for the moment, after what I had been through in the last year or so, I just wanted to have as much fun as I could! So I was very determined to find some, and I have to say, most of the time I did!

I spent a lot of my free time and some of my weekends one day with Gaby, of course by the water, getting the best tan I ever had; we Italians tan very nicely. That tan made me look real good in an off-white suit. Needless to say, the ladies liked the way I looked. The Castle Club Complex was now my habitual suburban weekend nightspot; their Diamond Lounge had a short food menu, of which I favored the ratatouille. After a number of frequent visits, it was automatically served to me, along with my favorite drink of the time, after I had been seated at a table in one of the raised sections on either side of the bar, which was located in the middle of the room. It was a good vantage point to see who was coming and going; being a regular had its benefits.

A Blissful Fantasy Interlude

On one momentous Friday evening, I spotted someone I thought I knew from my past.

No, sad to say, it wasn't Gail! Her, I would have had no trouble recognizing, although I was, from time to time, on the lookout for.

While hanging out with the guys, waiting on the Saturday-night babysitting with Patty, a young girl would frequent the store where we hung out in front of. She was a very attractive girl with long blond hair; about twelve or thirteen, I would say. Too young for what we all would have liked to have done with her. So, if this was her, and I was pretty sure she was, she was now a very pretty young woman with long blond hair, old enough to be with in the way I wanted to so long ago. Had to find out if she was who I thought she was.

Okay now, relax. I'll solve this mystery one way or another. You will have to bear with me for a moment; this has to be done with class. I didn't want it to look a common pickup approach, although it was a pickup, but not your ordinary one!

I composedly approached her, engaged her in conversation to inquire if she was the girl/woman in question. And to my pleasant surprise, she was! Now knowing who I was, she admitted she had had a secret crush on me back when she was that young girl but felt she was too young to do anything about it at that time and also knew I was Patty's boyfriend. Well, times have changed, and she wasn't too young anymore, and I certainly wasn't Patty's boyfriend now. We toasted to this reunion of sorts and spent what was left of the evening in each other's company, dancing and reminiscing about how things were back in our younger days. And when the club closed, she requested I follow her to her place to have a nightcap or a cup of coffee, whichever I preferred.

She had to work the next day, so in the morning, I just had some coffee and left. Not really interested in seeing her again, I just didn't call her, and neither did she call me.

As you can see, I was having some real good times and hoping it would last forever! I was the cat's meow, the balls, the man, etc., once again!

Playing by the Rules

One thing, though, that kept gnawing at me in the back of my mind was the question, how far would Deidre go to get what she wanted? With Deidre now calling me more frequently, asking if we could get together to go out for drinks and dancing, she was very persistent. In my effort to keep good relations with her, I figured, *What the hell, why not?* So we did. I took her to Waldo's in the capital city across the street from one of the tallest buildings there were at that time. I only went there on a date; the place was popular, small, and intimate but a little too noisy to be romantic. She wore red and looked like a million bucks!

We went for coffee after we left the club, some place quiet where we could talk. She told me she was getting out of the escort business and moving to a coastal city, mostly because she knew her mother was becoming too ill to take care of her daughter, so she would now try to get Gaby back, with or without my help. She needed to show the State authorities that she had a decent place to live, so they would approve of Gaby living once again with her mother. Deidre could then apply for State welfare assistance.

Just in case you're wondering, no, I didn't spend the night with her!

Once again, Deidre had appeared to have straightened out her act. So eventually, she was awarded custody of her daughter and financial help from the State welfare department. It wasn't long before she started giving me some difficultly about spending time with Gaby. She had her own set of rules I would have to follow; I will spare you the details. Let's just say she was starting to use Gaby for leverage, my guess was, to get me to commit to marrying her.

I would abide by her rules to be able to spend time with Gaby, but not go so far as to make the commitment of marriage. Now, it was a test of patience. She broke first by giving me the ultimatum that I must consign to what she wanted, meaning marriage, if I wished to continue spending time with her daughter, Gabrielle.

To buy some time, I told her I would consider it; she granted me this. I still was seeing Gaby because it made it more convenient for Deidre to have time for herself when Gaby was with me for the day. I played on this to give me more time, so much so that I even offered to take Gaby overnight if Deidre wanted or needed me to. She took me up on this a few times when she wanted to go out for an evening and not be concerned about coming home until the next day or to have some after-hours privacy at home.

I was hoping she would meet someone and it would take her focus off me so I could just continue spending time with Gaby for as long as she wanted to spend time with me. You see, I know from my own experience with my children that they reach a certain age when they would rather spend their time with their friends than with grown-ups such as parents, etc., because to them and their friends,

"it just ain't cool!"

Never really wanted to face that dilemma with Gaby; but as you can see, the way things were going, it was looking like I wasn't going to have to face that impasse!

Chapter Eight-Part Two

All Things Have an Ending

October 1989

OH YES, OCTOBER, the first full month of autumn. As a young boy, I liked October—the cooler temperatures after a hot summer, the smell of burning leaves, the anticipation of Halloween and, looking further ahead, the expectations of seeing family you only see at Thanksgiving, and then the best of all the holidays, Christmas!

I was so very unaware of the emotional distress I would suffer this autumn. I was so wrapped up in worrying about what might happen with my situation with Gabrielle and taking care of my business, I never expected what was on the horizon. Something I would never have wished for in a million years!

Late in October, on a dreadfully memorable rainy day, while executing my normal daily deliveries, my delivery truck began to a have a minor mechanical problem. The windshield wipers had stopped working; because it was raining, this wasn't so minor a problem. I immediately contacted my mechanic, Guy, who then instructed me to try a few things to see if I could get them working again. I tried everything he told me to do, but nothing seemed to get them to work! He advised me to bring the truck to him because I needed the windshield wipers to work so I could continue my day's work. On the slow and careful seven-mile drive to Guy's repair garage, I was somewhat upset; I preferred my days to go without troubles. Finally arriving at Guy's garage, he took a quick look to see if he could fix it right away, unfortunately to no avail.

"Jim, this looks more complex than I figured it would be. I might need some parts. You're going to have to leave the truck with me, and I'll get to it as quickly as I can. You might as well go home, and I'll call you if and when I get it fixed. It may not be today, but either way you'll hear from me. Come on, I'll give you a ride to your car," Guy proclaimed.

Okay, I'll be at home. Please let me know as soon as you can," I requested.

"I'll do my best for you, Jim!" he reassured me.

On my ride home, I knew I could always use my nonworking Wednesday to shift my schedule if need be. It would only be a minor interruption in my business week. Feeling this was the worst that could happen to me that day, I was now in for a very unpleasant surprise when I got home.

My older sister, Debby, and her husband's car was at the house. This was strange because they lived in the next state about thirty five miles north, and they would only come to the house on special occasions like birthdays, holidays, etc. This was a very disturbing discovery. Nevertheless, this created great anxiety for me! Something was wrong. I quickly made my way into the house. As I entered the back-entry door, I heard my sister call to me from the second-floor apartment back door.

"Jim, is that you?" she inquired, as she came walking down the stairs.

"Yes, it's me! What are you guys doing here today?" I answered her and asked.

"Well, bro, Mom wasn't feeling well and was taken to the local hospital. Dad called me, so we came down!" she sadly explained to me.

"What is it? What's wrong with her?" I anxiously questioned her.

"Jim, please, try to settle down. We don't know what her problem is yet!" she explained, in the attempt to calm me down.

"Why are you home already? Short day for you today?" she inquired.

"No, I had a mechanical problem with my truck and had to stop work to take it to my mechanic, Guy," I quickly explained.

"I'm going to the hospital and see if there's any news on Mom. I'll see you when I get back!" I persistently avowed.

I immediately called Guy's shop to tell him I would not be at home for a while and, if he calls about my truck, to leave me a message on my answering machine.

Through the Fire

As quickly as I could, I then changed my clothes and drove to the hospital emergency room to find out where my mother was. The registering nurse informed me that she had been taken to the sixth-floor intensive care unit.

I then headed there, thinking, *Oh man, the intensive care unit. That's not a good sign.*

The elevator seemed to crawl up to the sixth floor, or was I just imagining it? But it seemed to be moving at a snail's pace.

Finally, it arrived at the sixth floor, and I went immediately to the nurse's station to ask where my mother was and if I would be able to see her now.

"She's in room 8. There's a nurse in with her now, so I'm sorry, sir, you'll have to wait," the desk nurse informed me.

I stepped to the side near room 8 to wait, wringing my hands and feeling extremely anxious. I had hopes that it wasn't anything too serious.

It seemed like an eternity; whatever the nurse was doing seemed to be taking forever, until finally, she emerged from the room, asked me who I was; and in my telling her of my identity, she allowed me in to see my mom. I took a deep breath and entered the room. She was sitting up in the bed; this seemed like a good sign. She smiled at me and was troubled why I was here and not at work.

My mom, always concerned about others before herself. To me, she's an angel on earth! My best and most trusted friend, my confidant. She knew things about me that no one else knew and probably would never take the time and effort to learn! To me, she was the best thing in my life! I loved her unconditionally, eternally.

"Mom, what's going on? Have they said what's wrong?" I sympathetically inquired.

Before she could answer me, two nurses came in, and the taller one said, "That is exactly what we are trying to find out. And who might you be?"

"This is my handsome son, James," Mom proudly informed them.

"Okay, James, we need to take your mom downstairs for some more tests. She will be back as soon as we are done," the tall one explained.

"Well, Mom, you be a good girl for the doctors, and I'll see you when you get back. I'm going to the cafeteria to get something to eat," I declared.

Gave my mom a hug and a kiss and was on my way. Got directions to the cafeteria from the desk nurse. A lot was going through my mind as I walked to my destination, like it's too soon to lose my mom; she was only sixty six years old. I really needed to eat something, so I forced myself to do so; I needed to keep my strength up for what might be coming. It was mental torture to sit and think of what might be my mom's medical problem.

Finished my meal and went back up to the intensive care unit to find, to my dismay, she was not back yet.

I then inquired with the desk nurse on where she might be.

"Just a minute, sir. I'll try to find out what's going on," she sympathetically informed me.

Another eternity to wait for what I hoped would be good news.

But it wasn't very good news at all.

"Sir, she's going to be transported to the medical center in the capital city. We are not equipped for what care and treatment she needs," she kindly informed me.

"Thank you, but where is she right now?" I anxiously asked.

"You should be able catch them before they leave. Go to the emergency area now. They should still be there," she advised me.

I proceeded as quickly and as orderly as I could, really wanting to see her before she left. I was in luck; they had not left yet, thank you, God!

"Hey, mom, what's the trouble now? The doctors here aren't good-looking enough for you, so you're leaving?" I proclaimed, trying to make light of the situation.

She attempted to laugh but choked a little, coughing up what looked like blood into the plastic tray she was holding.

"James, sweetheart, I'll be fine. This is nothing. I'll be back home by tonight." Her honest attempt to fortify me with hope.

She was then carefully put in the ambulance for transport. Just before they closed the doors to go, I was able to say, "Mom, I love you, and I'll see you later!"

There wasn't any more for me to do now but go home and tell the family what I had learned. I didn't want to deal with my father on this, so I would inform my sister Debby, and she could tell him and my sister Valerie, who was now living with our parents.

With my father learning what had transpired, he immediately went to where they had taken my mom. We all followed suit as soon as we could to find out what the doctors had found, which turned out to be, she was suffering a massive heart attack. One side of her heart had blown open, so she was hemorrhaging internally. This meant they needed to get her into their OR as soon as possible to try to repair her heart and stop the bleeding.

God forgive me, I looked at my father and thought this should be happening to him, not her. My father signed some papers, and we all left for home. They would inform him of the outcome of the procedure as soon as they could. My sister Debby decided to stay at the house with our father until more information was known. That was good for me because I could communicate with her to find out what was going on. By late afternoon, they called to inform us that for the time being, they had patched her heart to stop the bleeding. She was now resting comfortably and would definitely not be coming home tonight.

Guy called me to tell me he had fixed my windshield wipers and put my truck back on the parking line. I could go back to work in the morning, and come morning, I reluctantly did.

I hurriedly but efficiently went through my day's work and got home just as soon as I could to find out what was going on with my mother's condition. Unfortunately, the news was not good; the doctors had called again to inform us that the patch had not held, and she has now in a coma and needed to be on life support.

Seeing my mother like this was a wide-awake nightmare. I spoke with one of the doctors involved, and he informed me that another operation would be too risky because the first operation's visuals and all the blood tests indicated that her major internal organs were about ten to twenty years older than she was chronologically. My mom also had her own version of an accelerated life! I asked him about an artificial heart or transplant; he sadly informed me that she was too weak to survive it.

The next call from the doctors was to tell us all to come into the hospital because all her major organs were now starting to fail her. It had now been four days and nights of sheer misery for me. It was now time to do something no one really wanted to do, and that was to give them permission to let her go. I hated to say it, but it was time to pull the plug. The hospital and doctors had now done everything they were capable of. We were all seated around a table in a room, waiting for the doctors to arrive. They informed us that there was nothing more they could do for my mother and laid a document on the table; it was the release to end the life support. My father and my sisters immediately got up and left the room, leaving me there to do this.

I asked once more in desperation, "Doctors, is anything more you could do for my mother?"

All three doctors shook their head no, meaning they had exhausted all their options!

Okay, *I* would have to let her go, so I signed the damn document and demanded to say my good-byes before they did this. They agreed and informed me that this would be done in the early-morning hours. I sadly made my way to her room. Everyone of my family had left the hospital, so I was alone with her. I didn't know if she could hear me, but just in case she could, I kissed her on her cheek and asked her to forgive me for anything I might have done or said that had hurt her and told her for what would be the last time that I loved her. I knew what her dying wish would be. You see, ever since the incident with DeeDee and my father, from time to time, my mom would request that I reconcile with him, so now I would grant her wish and muster up the strength to do it. It was the least I could do for the woman who was the best mother and friend anyone could ever hope to have had!

The wake and funeral, needless to say, was a heart-wrenching affair. The general undertone was that because I had signed the document to end the life support, I was a murderer! It bothered me a little, but knowing there wasn't anything more the hospital and doctors could do for her consoled me because no one in my family or nothing else was going to. Okay, I had now survived the worst loss of my life. The only thing I could get out of this was no one or nothing could or would ever hurt me this badly. I had thought that losing my bother had been the worst; this loss was a million times more heartbreaking than that was. I only had one brother, but you only get one mother. The hub of an Italian or any family is the mother, and everyone knows that when the hub is gone, the wheel falls apart; and ours did subsequently.

Spending any time I could with Gaby while I was going through my mother's ordeal and eventual death was extremely helpful for me. She had sensed there was something wrong in my life, so when my mother had died, I told her that my mother had gone to live with God and his angels and I would not be seeing her anymore.

"I'm sorry that you won't be seeing your mom anymore," she hugged me and sincerely said.

Gaby was the only one who consoled me and felt unhappy for me.

I truly believed that this was one of the reasons she came into my life. I had hoped that the way I explained it to her would help and comfort her when it became her grammy Rita's time to go.

Deidre, learning of my mother's demise, frigidly gave me her condolences. And then started to play hardball with the whole Gaby-and-marriage thing. Feeling I was emotionally weakened by what had just happened in my life, she would now give me her final ultimatum about the conditions for me to continue to spend time with Gaby. But she had made a fatal misjudgment in her thinking, for you see, what I had just gone through made me stronger. Surviving the loss of my mother made me realize that I was now strong enough to survive the loss of Gaby or anyone I had feelings for in my life, if I had to. In death, my mother had helped me as she had so often helped me in life.

I refused to marry Deidre and lost seeing and spending time with Gaby! It was okay. It really was because you see, it was more of a loss for Deidre and Gabrielle than it was for me. And maybe when Gaby got older, I would see her again. Sadly, to this day, I have not, nor do I know her whereabouts!

Thanks, Mom. I love you. Forever! So rest in peace, my dear, with your beloved son Joey. I think my sons and I are going to be okay! Because we will always cherish and remember all the love you gave us, along with all the kind and caring words of advice you had given to us while you were here.

The year 1989 finished off very cold and somber. The holidays were not as celebrated as much as they had been in the past. Although we all tried our best to be cheerful and in high spirits, without my mom with us, all the holidays would never be as jovial as they had been. But life goes on, and maybe with a good measure of hope and faith, there would be something in the future to compensate for the losses suffered in this past year.

End of Chapter Eight

Chapter Nine-Part One

By Its Cover

January 1990

Back to the Club Scene

IT'S NOW THE nineties! The beginning of a new decade, a new era, Deidre was now out of my life along with, sad to say, Gaby. I was about two years away from entering into my forties. I felt maybe I would contemplate finding a second wife, if somewhere out there was a woman that was well-matched with me. And Deidre hadn't quite fit the bill. The sex was great, but there wasn't enough depth of feelings on my part to marry her. I knew this wouldn't be easy, like trying to find a diamond in a large pile of glass! And sorting through all that glass, you get cut now and then.

I never had a problem meeting women, but that you already are very aware of. My only dilemma was I had not met the right one. It felt kind of bizarre to even think of being married again. I had been single for so long now and liked it. I would have to ask myself, was I ready to give up my autonomy once more? The one thing different about this time would be that it would be my choice and not some untimely incident that would decide for me, like my first time.

I would not focus on actually meeting a potential woman to marry; that would be the wrong way to go about it. More times than not, I have learned that the more you look for something in particular, the less you're apt to find it. It's almost like it knows you're looking for it, so it hides, and as an adult, I don't like playing hide and seek!

I would just focus on having some good times and see what happened, although at this time, I did promise myself two things: I would not be hanging in clubs at fifty years old or older; and if I had not found the right woman by the time I was sixty, if I make it there, I would stop looking for a second wife and just focus on doing some of the things on my "bucket list."

Okay, so much for all those thoughts of a second marriage. After all, I was only thirty-eight and still looking good. I was tall, dark, handsome, fit, trim, and a sharp dresser, so I'd been told by men and women alike. It was now time to try out my new suits and see if I could stir up some adventures!

1990 Early Spring

Half Blind Date

As usual, there were plenty of woman interested in being with me; the hard part was deciding which ones to be with. As awful as this might sound, I would play a little game with myself by figuring out what physical features and personalities or qualities I was most interested in and then date the ones that appeared to fit the bill. I knew this was very shallow of me, but hell, I was just out to have some fun. And if one of them seemed to have the potential to start a relationship with, than I'd give it a shot and see where it went. What made it somewhat difficult for me was that I was and still am a man who prefers to be and feel needed more than I need to be and/or feel loved.

Feeling needed made me feel loved, but for me, feeling needed had to come first!

The eighties—and it spilled over into the nineties—ushered in the independent woman who felt strongly that she didn't need a man the way they used to. With all due respect, most of them still needed a man, but not for as many things as they had in the past. So where did that leave a man like me? That wasn't a problem right now because the women in my life had very little potential to start a long-term relationship with. Oh wait, there was one I met who seemed to have some promise; she was the daughter of a female friend of my father's.

Go figure. My father trying to fix me up!

She was about my age, divorced with two young teenage daughters and lived about thirty-five miles south of me, in an old town by the water.

I was given her phone number and told to call her and discuss us getting together. She was agreeable to get together the very next Friday night. She, displaying a measure of caution in our initial meeting, requested that we met early in the evening somewhere public, and I accommodated her so she could get a look at me and take a little time to feel me out. That initial meeting had a small downside to it; she stated that I physically reminded her of her ex-husband; that was never a good thing, especially if the woman had had a bad breakup with her now ex-husband. With that being the only negative thing she could find with me, she agreed we should to go out for dinner. She wasn't the greatest looking woman I'd ever met, although she was attractive, but not really my type. She would fit into the category of women that resembled Cher, the singer, face and body. I followed her to her house—a nice single-family home with a pool in the backyard on a cul-de-sac.

I met her daughters and changed into my dress clothes, which I had brought with me in an overnight bag for the date, if it took place. Under the circumstances, I didn't feel I should get dressed at my house for a date that might not even happen, but it did happen; I had a strong feeling that it would. So we went out for dinner to a romantic waterfront restaurant, had a great meal and a good time in each other's company, one little incident that might be worth mentioning.

Wait! First of all, I was dressed to the nines, wearing an off-white two-piece suit, a light amber silk dress shirt, a black tie with a delicate gold scroll pattern, also my usual low-key bling—a gold pinky ring with a half-carat diamond, dress watch, gold bracelet, a one-quarter-carat diamond gold tie pin, and shirt collar chain with my two zodiac sign charms. (I'm born on the cusp of Libra and Virgo.)

On my visit to the men's room, there were two young gentlemen there, I'd say, about eighteen or so. One approached me and politely addressed me, saying, "Excuse me, sir. May I say, you're a real shape dresser. I want to dress like you when I get older."

All I said was, "Thanks, that's cool!"

When we got back to her house, she sensually requested that I stay the night with her. At this time, a very popular catchphrase was Just Do It, used by an athletic shoe manufacturer, so I did, and she requested that I stay until Sunday.

No surprise there, right?

(◊"Circle of One"◊ Oleta Adams)

During this time, I was still patronizing the Diamond Lounge in the Castle Club Complex. If I got bored in the lounge, I would go check out the Asia Room dance club that was just in the next room. That's where I would meet the next woman to have an impact on my life!

Anna

The following weekend on Friday night, I graced the Castle Club Complex with my presence once again as I was usually doing. Only this time, I skipped the Diamond Lounge and went right to the Asia Room dance club, not really having any high expectations, just to have a drink, mingle a little, and partake in a dance or two with a lovely lady or two.

It's usually when you're not looking, you find something. Or does it find you? Just some food for thought!

I was wearing my black double-breasted suit with a somewhat flashy shirt—dark amber with a collar that buttoned up tightly but comfortably around my neck; it had small gold chains that crossed in front of the buttons. I had my back to the bar, leaning against it, observing the dance floor when a lovely looking five-foot-tall woman, sort of resembling Madonna with black hair, came up to me and gently handled one of the chains and made a comment, saying, "What's this? Oh wait!"

And then she called to her girlfriend Anna, not too far from us down the bar. "Anna, come here and take a look at what I found!"

In her attempt to poke a little fun at me, her efforts fell flat. Anna then joined us.

The short girl pointed out my shirt to her. Anna commented to her girlfriend, "I kind of like it. Do you have a problem with it?"

"No problem. I just wanted you to see it," the short girl remarked.

Now with the ice broken with Anna, the rest would be easy, for you see, I really liked the look of this Anna and kept the conversation going by changing the subject to her name and apparel.

"So Anna, is it?" I inquired.

"Ya, so?" Anna defensively replied.

"Oh, nothing. I like your name. It seems to fit you, just as well as your dress does!" I appreciatively stated.

"And what's that supposed to mean?" she inquisitively answered.

"Mean, mean, it's supposed to mean that I honestly think you look terrific in the dress you're wearing!" once again complimenting her.

"Thank you, that's nice, because you'd look rather ridiculous in it!" she humorously replied.

We both laughed.

"Ya, I think you're right. What do ya say we dance and then exchange phone numbers and to see what happens?" I proposed.

"I'll think about the phone number exchange while we dance," she responded.

Wow, that was smooth, answering two questions with one answer. She sort of reminded me of me!

I liked Anna, who was about five feet four inches. Her hair, being light brown with blond highlights, was shorter than I preferred on a woman. Generally, I like it shoulder-length or longer. Hers just barely touched her shoulder, but hair does grow so that could easily change. She reminded of a young Bette Midler, full figured but in all the right places.

We danced; she must have liked dancing with me because we did the phone number exchange when we finished our first dance. We spent the rest of the time at the club in each other's company.

(◊"Kissing You"◊ Keith Washington)

When the club closed, I escorted her to her girlfriend's car that she had arrived in than began passionately kissing her good-night and boldly inquired quietly between kisses, "Are you sure you don't want me to come home with you, because it seems to me like you do?"

"I have entertained the thought, but not tonight. What would my girlfriend think of me?" she defensively replied.

I could tell she had a wall up, but not a very thick one. The kind that would easily crumble with a good measure of trust. Most of the time, a woman's trust problem with me was her trusting herself alone with me.

The next day was Saturday, and I did have plans to go south to see the one I recently met, went out to dinner with, and . . . !

The ride to her place was a little long, giving me plenty of time for thought. What were my thoughts about? Well, I was really not interested in having two women in my life at the same time, especially if I was going to "just do it" with both of them; I wasn't into that right now. So one would have to go. That's what my thoughts were about.

Pick and choose, pick and choose, pros and cons, pros and cons. Which one to be with? Which one to be without?

Feast or famine. I hated that! I really did! I'd rather just have one that was right for me!

Little did I know an event was about to happen that would determine that for me.

What's that Loud Noise!

Saturday afternoon was a beautiful day weatherwise, so we decided to take her daughters out for the day in her car—you know, a road trip. The day started out fine. She requested that I drive. After a day full of fun for everyone, on the way back to her house was where the trouble started. I had to drive on a road that had quite a few potholes. I hit one really hard, and yeah, you guessed it, the muffler fell off! Needless to say, she got very upset with me, as if I had done this on purpose; but she held back her anger with her daughters being in the car.

My thoughts were that she was overreacting. Once back at her house, she opened up on me with both barrels. Even though I offered to pay to replace it, she wouldn't quit! I, not wanting to get into this confrontation with her, just kept telling her that I would pay to replace it. After about forty-five minutes or so of her ranting, it seemed like she wasn't going to stop! So quickly and quietly, I grabbed my stuff and got out of there as fast as I could.

She had just made my decision for me! Now the road to Anna was open, hopefully no potholes or pitfalls. Having Anna's phone number in my wallet, I figured I'd stop somewhere to call her to see if she would like to get together that night. Real short notice, but what did I have to lose?

Pulling off the freeway, I located a pay phone, called Anna, and asked her out. Unfortunately for me, she informed me she already had plans.

"Okay, Anna, I know this was short notice, but figured I give a try anyway," I sadly stated and was about to say good-bye and hang up.

"Wait, Jim, how about we get together tomorrow? It's Sunday. We could spend the day in a town up north somewhere on the water," she suggested.

"Ya, that sounds like a great idea, and I know just the town. I'll call you in morning, and we'll iron out the details," I cheerfully agreed.

"I should be up about nine or so. Call me around then, okay?" she instructed.

"Ya okay. So bye for now. We'll talk with you in the morning!" I proclaimed and then hung up the phone.

Still have to get myself home, but tonight, what will I do? I'll just wait and see how I feel when I get home, and I still had about twenty miles to go. I decided to stay home and save my money for Sunday's day out with Anna. I was feeling good about seeing her, and it sounded like she wanted to see me as soon as she could, seeming slightly anxious.

My Feet Are Killing Me!

Our day out together was really nice. We spent it in an old town on the water north of her house. We did quite a bit of walking, then sat on some large rocks at the water's edge, and walked some more, taking in the sights and visiting the quaint little shops along the way. We stopped in a small café and had a nice lunch. At one point, she complained that she had not worn the right shoes for this and her feet were killing her, so I suggested that after lunch, we sit at the pier so I could give her a foot massage. She couldn't have been more agreeable to that idea.

Having done all the things we wanted and could do, we decided to head back to her house, which was in a city by the water also, but not as small or as old a town that we had spent our day in.

So within two days, I went from a woman in a southern town by the water to Anna, a woman in a northern city by the water!

At her house, we relaxed and talked a little about our lives. I was very interested in Anna's life. She seemed to have it all together.

Nice house, new car, fashionable wardrobe, and her furry friend, a golden retriever named Rusty a.k.a. Arnie short for Arniemal; plus she ran her own business, a home-party Parkway Jewelry resale operation. She seemed happy, but that was just a facade. When she finally opened up to me, I then learned what she was hiding about her life and what had recently happened to her.

It's a rather long story, so I'll try to condense it for you. She had been married, with no children, to a man she really believed she loved and that he loved her. She actually thought love and marriage were forever, wishful thinking on her part!

Unfortunately, her thinking like that made it harder for her to take when her marriage failed. As far as I could tell, she was not to blame for this breakup. Her husband had left her for an employee of hers that was envious of Anna's life, this employee thinking that Anna's husband was the reason for Anna's happiness and prosperity in her life. She could not have been more wrong; Anna's lifestyle was because of the hard work that Anna had put into it. You reap what you sow!

Because of these events, her self-esteem and trust of people were somewhat shattered. Also she was very leery of showing any emotions. I knew something about these matters and wanted to help her with hers. Sooner than she expected, she was feeling very comfortable with me, because when I mentioned I should be going soon, she suggested I stay the night!

Oh boy, here we go again!

It actually sounded good to me. I was a little tired and wasn't looking forward to leaving her. So I took her up on her invite and said, "Ya okay. That sounds great!"

"Jim, why don't you go take yourself a shower and I'll fix us a late supper," she implied and set me up with what I needed for a shower.

I showered, we ate, and I must say she was a good cook, then relaxed in front of the television. We had a little foreplay during the commercials, got too tired—or was it too excited—for television, and went into her bedroom for some sleep, of which we both got very little of.

I awoke rather early, had to get home, change my clothes, and get myself to work. As I was leaving her, she awoke and gave me a hug and kiss good-bye, saying, "Have a good day, honey, call me later."

"You have a good day too, and yes, I will talk to you later today," I replied.

So now I'm "honey," another pet name for me. That's okay. I liked Anna very much. What I didn't like was the way our first intimate encounter went.

The "Do Over"

(◊"Romantic "◊ Karen White)

I always believed first times should be extremely romantic. So I wanted a "do over." Anna wholeheartedly agreed. We planned this "do over" for the very next weekend. It was just what the first time should be—dim lights, soft music, wine, her fireplace roaring, and Anna dressed in a floor-length cream-colored lace and satin negligee that I had bought for us. Yes, for us, because she enjoyed wearing it and my eyes feasted on seeing her dressed in it.

The next morning, Anna had a peculiar look on her face. I asked what was up with the look on her face, and she answered me with

"Jim, hon, I really feel you have resurrected my emotions that I thought were dead in me, but I feel alive again with love, and it's because of you!"

"Anna, don't you think it's a little too soon to come to that conclusion?" I asked.

"Anna, before you answer that, please try to give this more thought and time. You have been recently hurt badly. Isn't that wound still fresh?" I reasoned.

"Jim, honey, what I'm trying to tell you is that by some wonderful miracle, you have healed my heart. I feel so alive again, more than ever," she wholeheartedly declared.

(◊"Emotions"◊ Mariah Carey)

Our relationship flourished. I came to have somewhat deep feelings for Anna. I would stay at her house just about every day and night. I so wanted to help her in any way I could, so I found things around the house that needed doing and I did them. I was her, as she lovingly put it, Mister Fix-it, from her heart to her house!

1990 Autumn

When her vendor, the Parkway Jewelry company, would come out with some new items every autumn, Anna would put on a fashion show in a large rented room in a nearby hotel for all the women that worked for her, selling Parkway Jewelry at house parties. This time, they had some men's items: a bola tie and a watch. She would get some of the women that worked for her to model the female things. Anna asked if I would please model the male items for the show. At first, I declined to do it. She was persistent in her efforts to get me to do this, saying that if I would do this for her, she would grant me almost any wish I could desire. She had two reasons for wanting me to model in her show: first and foremost, to show me off, because the woman who had stolen her husband would be there; second, to introduce the new items to a roomful of the women that worked for her.

She persisted until I finally gave in with the conditions that I do it my way and pick the music for it and that she make me a special dinner and serve it to me while she was wearing a very sexy and seductive black negligee that I would buy for her for the occasion. She agreed to my terms, so she had her male model! Anna had set it up so that I went on last, telling me that she was saving the best for last, a little sincere BS to give me courage, I supposed.

It's Showtime!

(◊"The Rush"◊ Luther Vandross)

The night of the jewelry fashion show arrived. I was a little nervous, but it was uncalled for because my performance was flawless. The song I had chosen was, "The Rush" by my man, Luther Vandross. The music began, I stalled a bit, so as to add a measure of mystery to who might be coming out next, entering through the double doors at the back of the room. Everyone turned to see who had entered, then I proceeded up the center aisle with thirty or so women in attendance. They began to scream as I entered, and they didn't stop until I was finished.

Like I was saying, I walked up the center aisle—dressed in a white shirt, black pants, and a black double-breasted leather suit jacket, the Parkway bola tie and watch—to the front of the room, where I stopped, made one slow turn, walked a little to my right then turned, and walked a little to my left, came back to the center, glanced at my watch, then turned it to the audience to show it to them, shrugged my shoulders as if to say, "Sorry, ladies, gotta go now," removed my jacket, slung it over my shoulder, and walked back down the center aisle, got to the doors, stopped, and suddenly turned and blew a two-handed kiss to all in the room. That got the loudest scream. Anna wasn't too crazy about me blowing the kiss, but she got over it soon enough.

We had a lot of fun spending the summer together—day trips, picnics, barbeques, and short trips and stay-overs to the well-known vacation spot to the south. And yes, some of these things included her family members and/or my sons. Our relationship seemed to be going smoothly. I did whatever I could to keep it that way. I really wanted and needed our relationship to flourish and be healthy.

The major holidays were approaching. She knew I had lost my mom the year before, so I told her it would be a little rough for me but I would do my best not to show it, in the chance that I might bring down the high spirits for everyone else.

There was one small humorous pre Christmas event worth mentioning!

I Should Put Honey On It

It was now time for Anna to once again drag out her Christmas decorations. Soon we would go and buy a tree. In looking through the things she had for decoration, she noticed that the Christmas stockings were old and her ex-husband's needed to be discarded and replaced. We went out that day, and one of the things we did was obtain new Christmas stockings. Back at home, Anna gave me the job of putting the names on them. I sat at the table, and she brought me the white glue and some red and green glitter to do the names with. I did hers, **ANNA**. She liked the way I did it and said,

"Okay, now do the one for you!"

I sat and thought for a minute or two, holding the stocking in my hands, just looking at it until Anna come over to me and asked,

Okay, why haven't you done the one for you yet? What are you waiting for, Christmas?"

"I'll do it, but I was thinking that maybe I should put *Honey* on it so you use it for anyone!" I humorously suggested.

She turned to me and sternly remarked, "Oh, that's real funny, not! You ass! Put **JIM** on it and stop foolin' around."

Then she kissed me and adoringly said, "Always the joker!"

March 1992

The Fatal Flaw

As happy as were and hoping for it to stay that way, there was one fatal flaw in our beautiful union: Anna had not had a child during her first marriage. I had learned a long time ago that it's just about every woman's dream to have at least one child of her own in her lifetime because that is what women were born for. It's the blessed and the best reason they are created for! I've always said that the carrying, birthing, and raising of a child is the hardest job on the planet. I would never want the total task!

But as demanding as it is, women have a strong instinct to do this no matter how difficult it is. Theirs is a measure of courage I do not possess, nor do I wish to or ever would want to! God has truly blessed them for having that valor, or none of us would be here!

Anna, being thirty-five years old, desired to have a child of her own soon; and knowing how strongly she felt about this, who was I to deny her of that? I now had the horrific task of telling her I had had a vasectomy a long time ago. This was not going to be easy, to say the least!

She broke open the subject by saying to me, "Jim, you and I have been intimate for a while now, and neither you nor I have been using any pregnancy prevention. That's a little risky, wouldn't you say?"

Knowing what I knew and she didn't, there was no risk at all.

Okay, I had to come clean on this because I did care about her too much to keep her in the dark any longer.

I was sitting at her dining room / kitchen table. I asked her to come and sit with me. I took her hand in mine and began to fess up. I gently began, "Anna, for good reasons of my own, and if you want to know them, I will tell you. I underwent a vasectomy a little while after my second son, Vincent, was born, when I was about twenty-two."

She then squeezed my hand a little to let me know she wasn't happy with this news.

"Jim, honey, please don't take this the wrong way, but you really should have told me this before our first liaison, don't you think?" she responded.

Not really knowing what I should say, I kept silent.

She continued, "Okay, so we'll just have to get it reversed, so that you and I can make a beautiful child together, hopefully that little girl you want but haven't had yet. After we're married, of course!"

Anna had a way of turning things to the bright side. She was one of those people that didn't give up on things very easily. She strongly believed there was always a way to get things done, which made her a very savvy and somewhat successful business woman.

I loved Anna enough to give this some serious consideration, not just pass it off as wishful thinking on her part. But the cost of the reversal operation, and with no guarantee that this would be successful. Anna and I staying together looked doubtful. She wanted the life she thought she was going to have with her husband, which was a lifelong marriage and a happy home with children, and who was I to stand in her way? I knew what I had to do, and it would not be easy.

Our split up was difficult for the both of us; we both had agreed it would be the only option left to us, mostly so she could have the things in life that made her feel happy and fulfilled.

To this day, I still believe that if Anna had had a child in her first marriage, we'd still be together today!

That was the first and hopefully the last time my vasectomy affected a relationship of mine in a negative way.

Chapter Nine-Part Two

The Undiscovered Country

April 1992

Triumphant Return

I WAS NOW feeling somewhat emotionally drained. What I needed to do was collect my feelings. I would preoccupy my mind with the day-to-day tasks of taking care of my business and my sons, the things in my life that still needed me, and I needed them. So I would take a few weeks and just chill out from the social scene. It wasn't too long before I got wind that my old stomping grounds, the Castle Club Complex was running a singles night on Thursdays, an event where mostly and supposedly single people of a mature age could meet, have a drink, and dance. I filed this information in my mind for future reference, figuring I might just check it out sometime in my near future, when I was feeling strong enough to chance another possible relationship of some kind.

In the meantime, what I really needed was to feed my ego and get my confidence level up once again, and the capital city clubs had usually helped me with that. I had also heard of a new club on the waterfront that was now the hot spot. It was now time to get myself back to the social scene that I had been away from, mostly to see if I still was appealing to women and find out if now being almost forty made any difference.

Okay, enough talking; time to get out there and test the waters, so to speak, starting at the deep end—the capital city clubs—so if things didn't go too well, I could wade into the shallows, the suburb clubs. Well, the deep end turned out to be no problem at all. The first night back in action, I ventured into the new club on the waterfront of the capital city. The waters tested better than I expected. As usual, I didn't have to do much more than look my best. Sitting at the bar, off to an area away from the main action, I ordered a drink, sat back to take a look around, and get a feel for the place, my usual MO in a new club. No sooner had I gotten comfortable than a very lovely, rather young, and very pretty blond woman about five feet three inches tall came up behind me and asked if anyone was sitting in the empty bar chair to my left.

I turned to my left, moved my hand, left and right, up and down, through the air, and said to her, "Well, the chair seems to be empty. Please feel free to sit and permit me the pleasure of buying you a drink," I chivalrously stated.

"Thank you, I will, but I'd like the pleasure of buying you a drink," she sweetly but firmly proclaimed.

"Thanks, that would be very nice. What's the occasion?" I inquired.

"Because you were nice enough to save me this seat," she answered.

"But I didn't—" I started to say, but she cut me off in midsentence.

"Just let me say, I really like your look and want to get to know you a whole lot better, if that's okay with you?" she seductively asked.

Her look and straightforward approach reminded me a little of DeeDee, so I started to feel very comfortable with her.

We talked about our lives, we were both single and free, danced a few times, and spent the evening at the club in each other's company.

When the bartender sounded the last call, I saw her frown, so I asked, "What's the matter?"

"I'm enjoying your company so very much, I really don't what this night to end. And it doesn't have to. I really would like it very much if you'd follow me home and have another drink or, if you prefer, a cup of coffee with me. Whata' ya say, darlin'?" she alluringly offered.

Darlin', ain't that a new one? You know, pet name for me!

So not wanting to make her feel rejected or disappointed, I agreed. I mean, after all, she was very attractive, sexy, and willing—not that it was ever hard for me to find women like this—so why not?

I couldn't come up with any reason why I shouldn't go with her. Can you? Well, I guess I was back in the game! So hang on tight 'cause here we go again.

Yes, as two consenting adults, we spent a blissful night of lovemaking, healing, for each other, any open emotional wounds we both had left in our lives at this time. This was a grand romance, but not an illustrious relationship. It only lasted about three weeks, and then a friendly mutual split up occurred for reasons I have now forgotten. But it was something we both needed to get from one another to be able to move on to whatever there was on our personal horizons. Sometimes, people have to help each other up so they can continue on their way through life. Please take note, this was a beneficial thing we had done for each other, and we were both very thankful to each other that we had met.

June 1992

I frequented a few more capital city clubs, and very similar incidences took place. Feeling this wasn't really getting me any more than rebuilding my confidence levels—kind of like spinning your wheels and not really getting anywhere—I decided to shift gears and try out the Thursday-night singles parties at the Castle Club Complex.

I adopted a more relaxed way of dress for this: dress shirt and pants, suit jacket, no tie, etc. It certainly was a different experience for me. I had thought I'd done it all; I could not have been more wrong. For some unknown reason, I couldn't get it through my head that there could always be something new on the horizon.

The room was quite large, with plenty of people in attendance, a wide age range—I'd say thirty-five to sixty was the range—appearing to be more of women than men. All these people were supposed to be single; I didn't think so! I got myself a drink and leisurely walked around, spending some time getting a feel for the place and atmosphere. Ended up hanging in an area that was less busy than most. As I leaned my back up against a wall at the far end of one of the many bars in the room, I observed a group of about ten or so people at the bar talking and laughing, just having themselves a good ol' time. I guess I had the appearance of someone who was feeling low, which was not to far from the truth, because a very handsome well-dressed older gentleman from this group glanced at me a few times and eventually addressed me. "Hey, my man, you look a little down. What's the trouble?" he inquired and walked two steps toward me to hear my reply.

"Well, thanks for asking, but it's a long story and you're having yourself a good time with your friends. I really don't want to intrude on you and your friends" was my reply.

"Okay then, if you don't want to talk about it, then please come and join us for a drink. What's your name?" he requested as he put his arm over my shoulder, leading me to the bar with him.

"Jim," I simply answered.

"It's good to meet you, Jim. I'm Victor. Hey, everybody, this is my new friend, Jim. Everyone say hi to him!" he announced and then made introductions all around.

For me, this really was a welcome difference from what I was used to happening to me in social scenes. Instead of meeting a new woman, I was meeting new friends. This was a welcome change, and most of the changes in my life were not. Victor seemed to be a nice guy with class. His favorite thing to do was to introduce people two each other. He would do this to me numerous times over the next few months. I would go to this singles night parties just about every Thursday night for a while and, on the weekends, patronize the capital city nightclub known as Il' Torinos, a five-floor complex with a café and bar on the first floor, a restaurant on the second floor, a live-band lounge on the third floor, and a dance club on the fourth floor with a fifth-floor balcony. This was now my social agenda. A few days during the week, and sometimes on the weekends, the new friends I had met at the singles party would hang out and enjoy the scenery at the waterfront. He had invited me to join them any time I felt like it. I was introduced to more people who didn't frequent the singles parties. Victor introduced me to numerous people, mostly women that he didn't actually know himself, at these Thursday-night singles parties. Some I asked out and some I didn't. Sorry to say, no one really memorable. The one woman that would be outstanding, I found without Victor's help! I must say, though, he had helped me get my confidence levels up to where they should be. As I became older and more mature, the ways of getting and maintaining my confidence levels changed!

Late September 1992

Deenie

(◊"I'm Calling You"◊ Marilyn Scott)

On one particular Thursday-night singles party, I was hanging at the bar I favored, scoping out the scene, when I spotted a woman that had one hand on one of the pillars in the room, dancing in place. To get a better look at her, I walked around to the other side of the bar and caught site of her profile, which looked very appealing to me. She resembled Rose McGowan, the actress. I then walked back to my original place at the bar. I thought for a moment of a way to break the ice with her. For some unknown reason, I felt this one needed a unique approach because, to me, she had an air of a very savvy woman that could spot what she felt was a player from a mile away. So my opening had to be humorous, honest, and somewhat original. It hit me like a bolt of lighting; I knew just what to say, so I walked up behind her and said, "Excuse me, but if you keep dancing in one place like that, you're going to wear a hole in rug or start a fire!"

"So why don't you ask me to dance so that won't happen?" she ironically inquired.

"Okay, I will. Would you do me the honor of dancing with me?" I gallantly requested.

"Yes, I would!" she pleasantly replied.

No sooner did we step on the dance floor than the song ended. Not liking the next song being played, we exited the floor. I then inquired if she would like to have a seat to have a drink with me and talk to get to know a little about each other. After all, we hadn't even introduced ourselves yet. Finding an empty table, we sat, and I looked her in her big beautiful eyes and introduced myself. "Hi, my name is Jim."

Just then, a waitress come over and asked what we would like to drink. We ordered from her and continued with our introductions.

"And mine's Deenie!" she informed me.

I was a little puzzled by her name; I had not heard it before. Seeing that I looked perplexed, she explained, "My full name is Geraldine. I was called Geraldeenie by my family, which got shortened to Deenie."

I really liked that she had a name I had not heard before; it made her appear very unique, and I very much liked unique!

This uniquely named, very attractive woman was about five feet five inches tall with shoulder-length very wavy dark brown hair, full lips, and a very pleasing figure. And like I said, she resembled Rose McGowan.

She was a year older than me. I had recently became forty; that made her forty-one on her next birthday, three months away. Oh, an older woman; not since my wife had I been with a woman older than me! But her name wasn't Mary, so I was okay with it.

I was hoping she wouldn't mind me being slightly younger than her, by nine months, because I was very interested in taking her out. So wasting no time, I asked if she'd like to go out for dinner with me this coming weekend. She agreed, but it would have to be Saturday night because she had plans for Friday night. I agreed, so we exchanged phone numbers, and she instructed, "Jim, call me Thursday night, and we'll iron out the details."

What she meant was to give me her address and what time to pick her up to go for dinner.

The club was about to close, so she gave me a friendly kiss good night and said that she'd talk to me when I called her. I put her number in my pocket, went to the bar where Victor was. He asked me how it went. I told him, "Good. She gave me her number and we made plans to go out soon." He was happy for me.

I then left also. Driving home, my thoughts were of this new woman and what might transpire from this meeting. She seemed nice enough, so maybe this will be a long-term relationship; I hoped it could be, but I would have to know more about her first. I was really getting tired of the one-night stands and short-term affairs.

What I felt I needed at this time of my life was someone I could try to build a meaningful relationship with.

Our first phone conversation was a very interesting one. After getting the details for our date to take place, we traded some past experiences in life. You know most of mine, so I'll focus on hers. Having older parents who were somewhat strict with her liberties—and it was my impression—Deenie was something of a wild child. Being an attractive healthy young woman, she liked to party as she wished. This conflicted with the way her parents expected a young lady to act. So in an effort to gain her independence, she married prematurely, the marriage only lasting about three years, producing no children. As far as I could tell, her last relationship didn't end well, which meant she was probably a little leery about a new one. A small barrier to get through! I decided to take her to an older restaurant, one of my mother's favorites, which was in a close northern suburb.

Funny thing was, when I first met Deenie, she was dressed slightly sexy—you know, a little revealing but not smutty; and when we went on our first date, she was dressed nicely but very conservatively: a dark colored dress with a high collar and long sleeves. Don't get me wrong, she looked great! It's just that, more often than not, women dress differently when they're on the prowl versus on a date, especially the first date.

My Black-and-White Shih Tzu

I arrived at the three-family house where she lived on the third floor at about seven thirty. I brought no bottle of wine on this date. She instructed me to ring the third-floor bell, and she would be down shortly. I heard a small dog bark but really couldn't tell where exactly it was coming from!

Our reservation for dinner was for eight; we were seated a little before nine. We had a very nice dinner and lingered in conversation over a bottle of wine, and then coffee and a shared dessert.

The time seemed to slip away; we realized it was getting late and that the restaurant employees were clearing away to close, so we would have to leave. It being too late to go on anywhere, I took her home, walked her to the door of the three-family house where she lived—in the city I had lived in for a short time during my marriage separation—entered the front door, and stopped at the foot of the stairs leading up to her apartment. I then heard the barking of what sounded like a small dog. She quickly exclaimed,

"Oh, that's Sammy, my black-and-white shih tzu, I'd better get up there and quiet him before he wakes everybody up," and she gave me a quick tender kiss and a firm hug! Thanked me for dinner and an interesting night.

I replied, "Thank you and good night!" then told her that I would call her soon.

She answered as she began to ascend the stairs, "Tomorrow wouldn't be too soon."

"Then tomorrow it will be!" I replied.

Then I quickly left so she could get upstairs to quiet the dog, and I headed for home.

Curious! My mind was clear, not cluttered with question; it felt good.

The next morning, I did have something on my mind. I had learned quite a bit about Deenie during our dinner conversation. Most important to me was that she was not interested in having a child at this time in her life; that was really good news to me. I believe you know why.

It now seemed to me that Deenie and I would be a really good match for each other because of where we both were in our lives at this time. The only thing that could spoil that was a personality clash.

Okay, so much for pre-analyzing our potential relationship.

Someone to Watch over Me

Our next date was the following Tuesday night. She had work the next day, so this had to be an early night. I took her to Il' Torinos in the capital city. During the week, only the café and bar on the first floor were open for business. Sitting at the bar, we each had a cup of coffee, with a shot of a favorite lacquer to drink separately or put in the coffee. I asked, "Are you hungry at all, they make a great gourmet pizza here."

"Thanks, but I had a late lunch today, so I'm not really," she related.

I suggested sharing a dessert between us.

She agreed and requested I pick one to surprise her with.

I decided on the tiramisu, one of my favorites, which she had never had before; she liked it very much!

She then requested that we leave soon; she did have to get up for work in the morning, so I accommodated her and we left. On the way to her house, she informed me that she was feeling ill, like she was coming down with the flu or something. She stated that she had not felt very good all day! By the time we arrived outside her dwelling, she really wasn't looking well at all. She needed me to help her up the stairs to her apartment. On the way up, she told me about her little dog, Sammy, that he wasn't too fond of men. I told her I usually got along very well with small children and animals, so she should not be too concerned. As we entered her apartment, Sammy came running to the door. I put my hand out to him, and all he did was lick it. Deenie was pleasantly surprised that he liked me!

She seemed to be getting worse. I suggested that I make her a cup of tea, that she take some cold medicine, and get into bed, and that I would stay the night to watch over her, just in case she got worse during the night. I would sleep on the couch in the living room so that if she needed anything, she could call to me and I would be there to help her in any way I could! She agreed, told me where to find a pillow and blanket.

I made the tea for her while she changed her clothes and got into bed. Returning with her tea, I placed it on her night table, told her not to hesitate to call on me if she needed me for anything. I believe she slept through the night because she didn't call to me at all. I know this because I didn't sleep much; if I did get any sleep, it was very light and sporadic, so I would have heard her if she needed me for anything.

I awoke to Sammy licking my hand that hung down alongside the couch outside of my blanket. He needed to go out, so I dressed and saw where she kept his leash. The spare door keys were hung up by the front door, which was very close to her bedroom, so I tried to be very quiet taking him out. Needless to say, Sammy seemed happy! When we came back, Deenie was awake. I asked her where she kept Sammy's food so that I could feed him and if she would like a cup of tea.

She answered, "You're such a sweetheart!" and then told me where to find Sammy's food and agreed to the cup of tea. I then put the kettle on for her tea and fed Sammy, then went to check in on Deenie to see how she was. While I was out with Sammy, she had called work to take a sick day. She told me she was feeling better, but was still taking the day off to be sure. Just then, the kettle sounded off that the water had come to a boil. I returned with her tea, placed it on her night table, and told her I had not slept very much. She then reached over to her right, pulled back the covers, and requested sweetly to me, "Get in here!"

I undressed to my briefs and got in under the covers with her. She was nice and warm; and we then embraced, began to kiss, and didn't stop until our lovemaking was blissfully finished!

Once again, it wasn't a first time that was very romantic, so to me, it needed a "do over." She agreed, and the following weekend, we took especially good care to fulfill that "do over" the way the first time should have been!

(◊"How Deep Does It Go?"◊ Carl Anderson)

Deenie and I would be spending three or four nights a week together; on these nights, I would stay over. We would spend the early part of the night watching television or a rented movie video. We were becoming close and building what seemed to be a very good foundation for a healthy long-lasting relationship. When I did stay over weeknight or weekend nights, my morning routine was to get up before Deenie; take Sammy out to do his thing and, after Sammy's walk, feed him back at the apartment; and get Deenie her morning cup of tea, no matter what the weather! Although Sammy, the little bugger, didn't like the rain, so I had to almost drag him to go and do his thing on rainy days. As you can tell, Sammy and I had become close buddies. Also, I finished my day's work before Deenie, so I would go to her apartment and tend to Sammy's needs. In doing this, Deenie could now come home from work and just chill.

Deenie and I had found some new-for-us activities such as live theater or dinner theater, local and/or professional; we took some road trips and weekend getaways—I, her, and Sammy!

Before we met, Deenie was spending her Friday nights at the Villagefair, another singles party held in a northern suburb establishment. She had not met anyone to date there, but had made some friends; and from time to time on Friday nights, she liked going there to see them. On these occasions, I would go to be with my friends at Il' Torinos in town. There was one particular guy, Joe, whom I had met there one night. We struck up a friendship, and we seemed to have a lot in common. The best part of hanging out with Joe was that, in appearance, we were the complete opposites. I was the handsome Italian Al Pacino look while he, the taller, was the good-looking English Roger Moore look! So there really was no competition between us when it came to women; they either liked my look or his. This made for a very comfortable friendship between Joe and me.

1993 Spring

But I Only Had Two Drinks!

On one of Deenie's Friday-night excursions, she asked me if I would meet her there after I did my thing in town. I met Joe at my club—that's right, my club. I was spending so much time at Il' Torinos, the manager, Michael, made me an honorary guest, where my first drink was on the house; and I was never charged an entrance fee. I asked him why he would do this for me, and he said, "I like you being in my club. You've got style, good taste, and you always dress to the nines. You give my place class, so I want you here as much as possible!"

So I hung with Joe for a while until he had met a woman and went off with her. That's when I decided to go see what Deenie was up to!

This place she was at was somewhat crowded. As I waded through all the people, trying to locate Deenie, I felt extremely overdressed with a suit and tie on. I spotted her on the far side of the dance floor, standing with a female friend. I approached her to say hello when she suddenly saw me and clumsily reached out to greet me with an embrace, and with slurred words, she proclaimed, "Hi, honey. What a nice surprise. Come on and dance with me!"

I could tell by the way she sounded and danced clumsily that she was drunk. I then caringly claimed, almost asking, "Deenie, sweetheart, you're drunk?"

"No, I'm not. I've only had two drinks!" she defended herself with slurred words.

"Ya, okay. Come on. I think you need to sit down," I claimed as I escorted her off the dance floor, almost carrying her.

No sooner did I get her to a chair than she sprung up with her hand covering her mouth and said, muffled and slurred, "I need the lady's room!"

Then she rushed off to it.

I had arrived there late, and the place was now sounding the last call. I sat near the lady's room, waiting for Deenie to come out. The place was emptying out; I gave it a few more minutes. Now the place was almost empty, so I decided to go in and find her, and I did—in one of the stalls, on her knees, driving the porcelain bus. I asked if she was done driving; she answered yes, so I gently picked her up and inquired, "Are you okay now?"

She wasn't too steady on her feet, so I half-carried her to her car, which I would drive to get her home, leaving mine there, that I would have to come back and get tomorrow. All the way to the car, she kept saying, "But I only had two drinks! But I only had two drinks! But I only had two drinks!"

I laid her down on the backseat and drove her home as gently as possible, finally arrived at her place where I had to carry her up to her apartment and put her to bed. She was still saying, "But I only had two drinks!"

"Ya ya, go to sleep now," I lovingly requested.

Then I undressed for bed, got in, and fell off to sleep.

In the morning, Deenie had a really bad hangover, the worst ever, she claimed; and I brought her a cup of tea and said, "Good morning, sweety, how ya doin'?"

"How do you think?" she softly and painfully asked.

"But you only had two drinks!" I playfully replied.

"Oh shut up!" she snidely but lovingly proclaimed.

"What you need is some food, so we'll stop for breakfast on the way to get my pickup truck," I sympathetically instructed.

She hesitantly agreed.

By midafternoon, she was feeling her ol' self again, which was good because we did have tickets to a smooth jazz concert in the capital city. I was very much into smooth jazz; my interest in this music started at the tail end of *my relationship with Anna*. Deenie was just starting to like it herself.

1993 Winter

This Present Really Sucks!

Christmas was now about three weeks away. Deenie's birthday was just about two weeks before it. I told her that I'd take her out for a birthday dinner this year and give her all her gifts at Christmas; she reluctantly agreed. My plan this year was to give her a "twelve gifts for Christmas" kind of thing, plus one gift for her birthday; she'd be getting all her gifts on Christmas Day, except one, which she would get on Christmas Eve. I divided the twelve between things that she wanted and things that she needed.

There was one thing she needed badly, and I knew she'd appreciate it but not be thrilled with getting it on Christmas Eve; but it was a rather large box, and I didn't want to bother wrapping it. So I brought it in, covered enough so that she couldn't tell right away what it was. I asked her to close her eyes and then open them to see that it was a new vacuum cleaner!

Not very thrilled, she said, "Thanks, I appreciate it, but not on Christmas Eve!"

"Well, it's too big to wrap and put under the tree, so I gave it to you now. I know you think it sucks to get this on Christmas Eve, and it really does suck—it's a vacuum cleaner—but you really needed a new one! I promise you're going to like the other things we'll be getting tomorrow morning," I gratifyingly explained.

1994

Now with the holidays behind us, we could get back to spending time together, doing the things we had come to enjoy.

We spent the year trying to strengthen our relationship, but like most women, I believed Deenie expected it to go to the next level, and that was for us to get engaged. During the year, we had a few disagreements that caused us to break up a few times; but somehow, we would patch things up and get back together. Our relationship was becoming stagnant for Deenie; she wanted more, and I was very doubtful about going to the next level. Unseen tension was growing between us; they were starting to show by us having more and more disagreements about small things, and Deenie's mood swings weren't helping. Nevertheless, we made it to the next year together.

1995

(◊ "Miracle" ◊ George Howard)

I really never thought we had much time left together. Most of the years were uneventful, just going along being and doing things together and trying to enjoy each other's company, but toward the end of 1995, an event would take place that would break whatever was holding us together. Well, at least, it would for me. Deenie's father had a health emergency and ended up in the local hospital.

Things weren't looking good for him; I couldn't quite understand why it bothered her so much because she had never spoken very highly of him.

She was now visiting him every night and expected me to go with her every time. I told her I was having a really bad problem with this; it was too reminiscent of what I had gone through with my son and mother recently. I walked away from her during this time, which I knew would be unforgivable, but I couldn't find the strength to be there for her constantly. I knew what she would feel because it had happened to me before with Deidre.

1995 Early Winter

This breakup was the final one; there was no getting back together this time, and I resigned myself of even trying. I was emotionally weak but hopeful that something better would be coming into my life. So as usual, I went back to the club scene to find a distraction and get past this. The only one who seemed to be happy about all this was Joe. He was glad to have his clubbing buddy back, and he'd be playing an intricate part in my events in the future. It's said that everything happens for a reason, so there must be something new on my horizon! And it wanted me to be available for it.

End of Chapter Nine

Chapter Ten-Part One

Love's Labors Lost

The Buddy System

OKAY, SO I'M footloose and fancy-free once again, and as I said, Joe was happy to have his clubbing buddy back! Just in case you don't know what men do for each other in the club social scene, I'll fill you in. When a woman is checking out a man visually from across any distance of any size, and he looks in her direction, she will instantly look away. But when his buddy looks at her, she won't look away, so the one that she's not interested in tells his buddy that there is a woman checking him out. Providing he likes the look of the woman that's been checking him out, this makes for an approach that will most likely be a positive one. Because he now knows that she is attracted to him and somewhat interested in meeting him.

First contacts should be simple and straightforward, no stupid pickup line. Just introduce yourself with your first name, and if she responds by giving you her name, you should then have the courtesy of buying her a drink or asking if she would like to dance. If she accepts either or both, you have now accomplished a successful first meeting!

The other thing a club buddy is good for is he provides you with a home base so that when you venture out to make contact with someone and it doesn't go too well, you will have a place to return to with a friendly face, so you can recoup and try again.

Also, as a base, he provides you with someone to check in with as a reason to be excused from the presence of a woman you've recently met, if she turns out to be somewhat undesirable to you, for whatever reason.

A gracious retreat, for instance.

"You'll have to excuse me. I need to see what my friend is up to."

I would surmise women do something similar for each other. However, with a group of women being more like a safe haven than a home base.

Busting with Pride!

At Il' Torinos one momentous evening, I had an encounter with the women's group "safe haven" thing. I had met a very lovely woman about five feet two in height with shoulder-length wavy black hair and a knock-out figure. She was being extremely physically passionate with me. In other words, she really liked to kiss and play touchy-feely with me on or off the dance floor. I had no problem accommodating her, somewhat within the acceptable limits in public. She was all over me like a cheap suit. I had no objections, but her group of girlfriends did. We spent what was left of the evening in each other's company. When it became time to leave, I walked her outside to where her group of girlfriends were waiting for her. She was still being very clingy, so her friends had to gently draw her away from me, and one of them turned to me, declaring,

"She's not going home with you!"

"I wasn't expecting her to!" I plainly replied.

She had given me her phone number, so I'd leave it for another time. Little did I know, at this time, that this woman had something I had not encountered yet.

Just when I think I've seen and done it all!

A few days later, I called her, and we made a date for dinner. It was a pleasant enough evening. When I took her home, she invited me in for coffee. I was unaware at the time, but she had something she was busting to show me. I made myself comfortable on the couch. She had gone to the kitchen; she claimed to make some coffee for me. I was keeping my overcoat on, trying to be a perfect gentleman. She reappeared, wearing only an animal print silk camisole top and tape panties. She stood facing me, very close, which made her breasts level with my face. She then lifted her camisole top in order to expose her enhanced breasts to me, inquiring, "So what do you think? Don't they look real and natural? Come on, don't be shy. Feel them, and see for yourself!"

Not wanting to disappoint her, I felt them and told her, "They look very real and feel very natural!"

She then straddled my legs, kneeling in front of me, pressing her beast in my face. With a muffled voice, I requested her to let me get my overcoat off. She slid back and stood up. I then stood up to remove my coat, and she put her hand out to me in order to escort me to her bedroom.

In the morning, she gave me a man's silk robe to wear while I ate the breakfast she had made for me. After I enjoyed breakfast, I told her I needed to go home to change my clothes and that I would call her later if she liked. She agreed to me leaving and calling her later.

On the way home, I just couldn't get over how she had displayed her breast to me, as if they were a new car she had just bought and wanted to take me for a ride in! The ride she did take me on didn't feel anything like a ride in a car at all. They really were something, and she was busting with pride about them! I must admit they did look and feel very real; if she had not told me, I would not have guessed that she had had a bust enhancement.

We dated a few more times, and I came to realize—by some of the things she would say regarding her life, wants, and needs—she was looking for a man with money so she could quit her realty job and she would live off him. Therefore, I stopped calling her and started looking for someone else. After coming out of that adventure, I just couldn't imagine who or what might be next in my life!

What I found was a somewhat difficult and problematic relationship.

Okay, hold on! Here we go! Remember what I said about what happens just when you're not looking?

1995 Late December

Cheryl

(◊ "A Matter of Time" ◊ Pamela Williams)

Yet another momentous evening at Il' Torinos was due to the fact that my buddy Joe was very attracted to women with an Asian look to them, simply because his ex-wife was a woman that had these looks. I'm telling you this so you will have a clear understanding of the circumstances of how I came to meet Cheryl.

Cheryl had come to Il' Torinos and was hanging with an Asian-looking female friend. Joe spotted this Asian-looking female and immediately was interested in meeting her. Seeing that she had a girlfriend with her, he then touched my arm, a signal to follow him to their location. His approach was always simple and direct—a first-name introduction and then getting hers.

With that accomplished, he danced with her, which left me alone with the girlfriend, Cheryl. I really wasn't interested at this time in meeting someone new to date. Cheryl was thirty-five years old, five feet three inches, and had very short light-brown hair and a few extra pounds; she resembled Jamie Lee Curtis, the actress. She wasn't actually the type of woman I was usually attracted to, because to me, short hair gives a woman a somewhat masculine look.

It was just after Christmas, and people were anticipating New Year's Eve; and as usual, Michael, the club's manager, had given me two free invitations to the club's New Year's Eve celebration! I had no women in my life to accompany me, so I'd just give one to Joe and we'd go stag. News Year's Eve presents a great opportunity to meet someone new!

Okay, back to Cheryl. With her friend gone off to dance with Joe, she turned to me to strike up a conversation by introducing herself, saying, "Hi, I'm Cheryl."

I took this as her just being friendly and nothing more because I was doing my level best to ignore her while looking for who might be in the room that had more appeal to me or just someone to go and talk to. Not finding anyone in sight, I broke down, turned to her, and displaying no real interest, said, "Ya ya. That's nice. I'm Jim."

"Jim, you seem upset about something. Do I dare inquire if you would care to talk about it?" she noted and asked.

"Well, it's about my relationships with women. No matter how hard I try to keep them together, something always comes up to tear them apart. It's very frustrating and disappointing. I've just about had it with them," I explained.

"You shouldn't just give up on relationships altogether. It's probably because you haven't met the right woman yet," she proclaimed.

"Oh, believe me, I've met lots of women. You'd think I'd have met the right one by now," I claimed, in an effort to dissolve any interest, she my have had in me.

"So you've met many but not the right one yet. Sounds like quantity, not quality. That doesn't mean you should give up on finding Ms. Right," she stated as she looked me straight in the eye in an effort, it seemed, to present her self as Ms. Right!

She seemed to be making a little sense. I began to drop my defensive front a bit and I asked her, "Do you think you could be my Ms. Right?"

"Well, why don't we find a quiet spot, have a drink or two together, and discuss the possibilities," she suggested.

Well, maybe she wasn't physically my type, but she had a way about her that was starting to interest me, and maybe the change would do me good.

Remember, I said maybe!

Our conversation began with me asking her where she lived.

She told me she owned a small one-family house about twenty-five miles south of the capital city. She lived there with her eleven-year-old daughter, which she had from a boyfriend that she decided not to marry after she found out a few things about him that he had kept well hidden from her and that she decided she didn't want to deal with. For the sake of discretion, I won't go into any details.

Before living where she was now, she was living in the next city just southwest of me. She had a good job with a company that more or less leased and maintained computer programs for companies to use in their day-to-day business operations.

It seemed that we were now enjoying each other's company. She had made a small crack in the shell I was in, so I wanted to do something for her at the first opportunity, and I didn't have long to wait.

Going South with a Stranger!

The evening seemed to fly by. Before we knew it, they were sounding the last call so it was time to leave, and we had exchanged phone numbers then agreed that we would talk on the phone about getting together in the near future.

Therefore, I escorted her to the coatroom, where I helped her put on her coat then asked her, "Where did you park your car?"

"Just up the street, one block on the first side street on the right," she informed me.

"Okay, may I walk you to it?" I requested.

"Sure, if you'd like," she answered.

While walking her to the car, I questioned her about how many drinks she had had and if she was okay to drive home alone and then somewhat jokingly suggested I go with her for safety's sake, actually expecting her to say no. She surprised me by saying yes! I saw Joe outside the club, waiting on the valet to get him his car. Went over to him to tell him what I was doing. He just shook his head and said, "You sure you know what you're doing, Jim?"

"Ya ya, I'll be fine. I'll call you tomorrow," I exclaimed.

Got into Cheryl's little foreign car and headed south with a stranger! I found out later that about halfway to her house, she was having second thoughts about this arrangement, but it was too late by then to turn back, so I guess she decided to make the best of it. Just before we arrived at her house, I inquired, "So is your daughter home with a baby sitter?"

"No, she's staying at my aunt's house for the night," she enlightened me.

Her aunt's house was north of my house, so she knew she'd be going north the next day to get her and to also to bring me home.

Sounded like a well-laid-out plan to me, wouldn't you say? Nevertheless, she'd never admit to it!

"So we'll be alone," I stated innocently just as we pulled in the driveway.

She unlocked the side door to her house, we entered the kitchen, she then pointed out that the bathroom was the first door down the hallway to the left and that her bedroom was the last door on the right and that her daughter's room was at the end.

Off the kitchen, there was an archway leading into the living room, and a door halfway down the hall on the right led to the den, a small room where she had a small couch, computer, and television.

Oh, Am I in Trouble!

"So your bedroom's down this way?" I said as I pointed down the hallway and started to walk toward it.

"But the large couch is in the living room!" she informed me.

"That's nice, just where it should be!" I said as I flopped on her bed.

In her effort to display to me that she's not an easy woman, she protested, but not very strongly, about me being on her bed. I then stood up, gently embraced her, and reminded her that I was stranded here at least until morning and that we were two consenting adults, so why not make the best of it? And then I sensually kissed her, and she seemed to melt in my arms.

As I was kissing her neck, I just barely heard her softly sigh, "Oh, am I in trouble!"

Though she meant it as the kind of trouble that you don't mind being in. We spent a very blissful first night together!

In the morning, we went out for a late breakfast; she had the luxury of a change of clothes while I had only the clothes I wore to the club for the night out. It was now getting close to noon, and she would have to get going north to pick up her daughter. And so we got in her car and headed north. She dropped me off at my house first, so meeting her daughter would have to be another time, if at all. It seemed all part of her plan!

Exiting her car, we agreed to be in contact soon. We said our farewells. I changed my clothes and called Joe to let him know I was home and to talk to him about next weekend's Il' Torinos New Year's Eve party. He was very agreeable about us going stag. Cheryl and I didn't make contact until the end of the week. I really wasn't sure what to do with this potential relationship. I had my doubts, because she lived so far away from me and a few other things I won't go into right now. I just needed some time to think!

The club's New Year's Eve celebration was quite lavish. Food, champagne, hats, noisemakers—you know, the complete New Year's layout! Joe and I had been there for about an hour or so, standing on the fifth floor, observing who might be there. Facing me, Joe gave me the heads-up that the woman I met last time we were here was coming up behind me. I slowly turned and showed my surprise that she was there.

"Hi, Cheryl, why didn't you tell me you were coming to this? Did you pay to get in?" I inquired.

"The subject never came up in our conversations, and yes, I did have to pay to get in!" she replied.

"Well, that's too bad. If I had known, I would have left your name at the door, and you wouldn't have had to pay," I explained. Cheryl had come with a small group of her female friends, and of course, I had to be introduced to them while Joe avoided it by quickly talking to the first woman he could find.

Cheryl made a point of the fact that she hadn't brought her car with her this time, I suppose to give me the idea of taking her home so that we could spend another night together. I wasn't too sure that I wanted to. Therefore, I would leave that until later; there still was a lot of night to go through yet. I hung with Cheryl for most of the evening, having drinks, a little dancing, and some conversation. It now seemed to me that Cheryl wanted more out of this than I did, so after our New Year's Eve liaison, I started to back off.

(◊"Until You Came Back to Me"◊ Basia)

Cheryl started to pursue me by coming by my house, making a barrage of phone calls. I finally broke down and opened up the line of communication with her, telling her we needed to slow it down a bit. It was to no avail; she just came on stronger, making plans for us to do things together like day trips, picnics, etc. A few of these plans included her daughter, who viewed me as a threat to the tight mother-daughter relationship. With no father in her daughter's life, Cheryl had overcompensated for the absence, which had made their bond so tight.

Cheryl had lost her mother when she was a very young girl; her father messed with the situation and only skewed up things. Cheryl ended up living with her mother's sister, which was the best thing that could have happened to her, from my point of view. Her aunt was an extremely wonderful person. With a large family of her own, she took in Cheryl and her siblings—two sisters and her bother—for a while. He eventually went and lived with their father. Really didn't know much more than that and didn't want to. For this reason, Cheryl was very much family orientated, which for me would become a problem.

Okay, so Cheryl and I had started a relationship, and at the beginning, it was a real good one, but aren't they all at the beginning? Her house needed some repairs and/or fixes, for example; all her electrical receptacles only accepted two-prong plugs, and most things that needed electricity had three, so I told her I would change them all if she bought them.

Another thing I found to be wrong was that all her telephone extensions were on long phone cords that ran up and down the hallway, making it very difficult to vacuum the hallway. So once again, I told her if she would purchase what I would need to fix this, I'd do it the right way, which I did. Just a few of the many things I fixed and/or repaired for her in the house. Because I was able to do what needed to be done, she saved quite a bit of money, not having to hire someone for these things.

1997 Summer

You Don't Have a Patio!

One day, while out shopping at a local emporium, I found Cheryl checking out some patio furniture, and I asked, "Why are you looking at patio furniture? You don't have a patio."

She looked at me, smiled, and said, "But I could have one!"

This was another instance where I should have kept my month shut about the things I'm capable of doing and my knowledge of construction. When would I ever learn?

Another noteworthy tidbit: It was about this time, I got sick of having a pager and stopping to call people who have paged me. I acquired my first cellular phone; that way, personally or in my business, people could now reach me direct.

I told her to get an estimate from a local contractor about putting in a patio; the quotes she got for a nine-foot-by-nine-foot cement squares patio were ridiculous, such as twelve hundred dollars.

I then suggested we could do it ourselves for a lot less, and we did. Hence, she got her patio furniture.

Another time my knowledge of fixing, repairing, and constructing things paid off big-time was on a cold winters' night when her street was icy. A car slid up over her front lawn and took down the mailbox we had just put up and made a large scar in the lawn. The next day, we found the car parked in a neighbor's driveway, and I confronted them to find that it had been their teenage son who was driving the car. Being now able to name the perpetrator, her house insurance would award her the damages with no problem, after an estimate from a reputable local contractor. Of course, I would fix the damages and with the money she received, we took a five-day trip to that favorite southeastern vacation area.

As time went on, things would start to deteriorate mainly because her family, friends, and daughter kept coming between us; and the general problems of having a daughter approaching puberty made things even worse. Another thing I started to realize was that the only time she came close to looking at me as number one in her life was when we were off on our own, away from all the things that took her time, energy, and attention away from me.

After all those things, then came me! I wasn't even second fiddle; I was more like sixth or seventh most of the time. In an effort to try and salvage our relationship, I would as much as possible take her away on weekends with me, mostly to that generally popular vacation spot in the southeastern part of my state. These were the times I'd be number one, although her daughter, once learning of our whereabouts by Cheryl calling to tell her in case of an emergency, would call for no other reason than to get between us. I wished I could have done this every weekend, but it would be too expensive for me because, most of the time, I was footing the bill. It must be made clear for you to know that Cheryl and I had what I'd describe as an, "on again, off again, in and out of each other's lives" relationship over a period of about ten years. On occasion, our bond was so fragile, small things and simple words could cause us to split up! I must point out that arguments and disagreements between Cheryl and me never got out of hand and on no account came even close to getting physical. I can't say the same for the ones between Cheryl and her daughter, unfortunately!

March 1998

For a reason I have long forgotten, we had such an intense break up at this time that I felt like it would finalize your relationship. Looking at it that way, I had planned to get myself back out in the social scene, so I made contact with Joe, in which I wasn't sure how he would react after my long absence. However, like a good friend, he wasn't fazed by it much; and we went back to our old routine. Needless to say, a lot of people were glad to see me again and I to see them! Although, I had an eerie feeling that something profound was on the horizon.

Always a Woman to Me!

May 1998

Hanging with Joe at Il' Torinos actually felt good, and everybody there who knew me was happy that I was back, especially the manager, Michael, who welcomed me back warmly! Nothing seemed to happen right away. That was good; I really needed to ease my way back into this scene. Too much too fast wasn't a good thing. I was trying to stop things from happening too fast anyway!

I was now at a point where I wasn't even trying to meet someone new. I would still have the occasional women come up to me and try to make conversation; most of time, I would just blow them off as pleasantly as I could.

But there was one night of a subconsciously anticipated event I had given up on years ago. Just a little before closing, I was leaning up against the wall to the left of the fourth-floor entrance/exit to the stairway that allowed access to all five floors, just minding my own business, killing time, enjoying my drink, just taking in the sights and sounds. Joe was sitting at Maryann's bar a few feet to my right, having a drink and talking to a woman.

Just about then, a well-dressed woman sauntered up to me. She seemed a little unsteady on her feet, a few too many drinks perhaps? She wasn't tall enough to look at me eye to eye; she stood on tiptoe and still wasn't tall enough to accomplish it, but she gave it a good try. She stood in front of me, very close. My shadow blocked the light from above the entry way and kept it from fully illuminating her face, so I really couldn't tell what she looked like, but of what I could make out, she was attractive. She placed her hand flat but gently on my chest, as if to hold me against the wall.

By the way, if someone you have just met physically touches you, it's a sure sign they like you and feel very comfortable with you!

Her opening statement came in the form of a slightly slurred sarcastic question.

"So what's your story?"

"How much time you got?" I answered in a clear voice, challenging her.

As I waited for her answer, she moved slightly to her right. The light from above the entrance illuminated her face, and I believe my heart actually skipped a beat! I thought to myself, *"Oh my god! Could it be?"* After all this time? I had just about given up on this ever happening!

My thoughts were racing through my mind; my heart had a quickened pace. I was sure, with her hand on my chest, she could feel it. My mouth had gone dry, so before I could say anything more, I had to take a sip of my drink that was almost finished. If she was who I thought she was, I had to keep my cool, not come on too strong, and most of all, be gentle. It felt as if a butterfly had landed in front of me, and if I made any sudden moves, it would fly away and be lost to me once again! All this passed through my mind and body in a matter of seconds.

My undying elusive butterfly of love?

As my mind filtered through my racing thoughts and I became more lucid, I realized it was her. A little older, sure, but it was her!

All I could say to her came in the form of a question.

"Gail?"

She looked at me with a slightly puzzled expression on her face, and replied, "Excuse me?"

Not sure if she had heard me or was just stunned by me knowing her name, I replied slightly louder and added her last name.

"Gail—?"

I then said my first name and repeated it, adding my last name in an attempt to confirm my identity.

"It's me, Jim. Jim—!"

She then gave me a long hard look and, in the instant, she realized she recognized me, slapped my face, and cursed me, "You bastard!"

In that same moment, she threw her arms around me, and we kissed with an immeasurable degree of emotion; she then began to cry. I hoped it was with the happiness of us stumbling on each other after twenty years! As the sting of her slap dissipated, my thoughts started to race once more, with all the questions I had held inside me for twenty years and finally getting the chance of a reconciliation I had prayed for and a possible second chance at our relationship with a more mature approach this time!

Our long passionate kiss ended, and we looked deeply into each other's eyes, both realizing there was a lot of catching up to be done. The first thing I could think of was to ask her to go to the bar, sit with me, and toast to this—what I felt was a long-anticipated, wonderful occasion and, hopefully, a reunion. I didn't really know if it would, but I wanted it to go beyond this brief encounter. It was late; I asked Maryann, the bartender, if I could order drinks for myself and Gail, a woman from my past I had not seen in twenty years. She began to explain that the last call had already been sounded then stopped and said, "But for you, Jim, under the circumstances, I guess I could make an exception. And it's on me!"

Gail looked at me, somewhat impressed, but impressing her in this manner was not my intention. I then suggested that, tomorrow being Saturday, we have a lunch date and catch up on what had happened in our lives in the last twenty years.

To my surprise, she refused my invitation for lunch and insisted that we go to her place that night, which was not far from where we were, and do the catch-up. My attempt at the mature approach wasn't working, so I reluctantly gave in to her desire to do this now and not wait until tomorrow.

Please believe me, I was not expecting anything more than talking with her over a cup of coffee about a possible second chance for us and finally having the long-awaited and anticipated chance to tell her that I loved her then and still did now!

I had come to the club in Joe's car, so I needed for him to take us to her place. After a short but sweet explanation of who she was to me, he had no problem accommodating us; as a matter of fact, he was somewhat amused and happy for me by all this.

My plan was that Gail and I would have coffee and conversation to make plans to get together as soon as possible and that I would than take a taxicab home.

But as you already know, "the best-laid plans of mice and men often go astray!" Besides, Gail had her own plan!

And this plan of mine could not have gone any more astray than it did. Like I said, and you must please believe me, what happened that night/morning—after all, it was about two thirty Saturday morning.

Why do we always assume that just because it's dark outside, it's nighttime?

Anyway, what happened was in no way my intention of what had or should have taken place!

We arrived at the front door of her apartment building in the lobby. I made one last attempt at my idea of a lunch date for Saturday, but she insisted it be now. I gave in to her insistence, asked for a moment to tell Joe that I'd be staying here for a while so he could go. He wished me well and took off. Back in the lobby, Gail had the door open, so we went up to her place, entered; and she requested I make myself comfortable on the settee while she made the coffee in her alcove kitchen, where I could see and hear her through the open space that was above the breakfast counter. I was still feeling amazed at what had happened; however, I was extremely happy that it did. I silently thanked God for this, for many times I had wished that he would grant me this encounter.

Finally, having this chance to admit to her my feelings then and now, I did. She came from the kitchen, straddled my legs, and replied that she felt the same. And then she began to unbutton my shirt enough to put her hand inside. Moving it slowly and softly on my chest, she sensuously said, "It's been a long time for us, baby, and you still look as good as ever."

"And so do you!" I replied.

We intensely kissed! She then slowly got up and headed to what I figured was her bedroom, saying, "Relax, baby, I'll be right back!"

She reappeared with and wearing something she remembered from twenty years ago that was and still is a turn-on for me.

"Like I said, and so do you, Gail!" I repeated with great anticipation of what was to come.

I believe you can now tell where this was all going, so I'll stop right there and just say we had an incredibly *hot and heavy* multi-bliss-filled encounter! It was truly amazing, like the twenty years was just yesterday, and we picked up just about where we had left off so long ago; but instead of refusing to stay the night with her, I accepted. It goes without saying I didn't get much sleep at all.

At daybreak, we had that coffee intended for our talk earlier. I then requested that she accompany me to lunch but first take me to my house so I could change my clothes.

Second Chance?

During lunch, she informed me that in the twenty years between our liaisons, she had not married, nor did she have any children. Amazed at this, I had to ask her why she had not. She sadly replied, "Well, baby, it's not like I hadn't come close. But when I did, I'd remember my love for you and couldn't go through with it!"

Hearing her call me baby warmed my heart almost to a boil!

"I am sincerely sorry!" was my heartfelt reply.

"And, baby, what about you?" she asked with bated curiosity.

"Okay, five years after we split up, I got divorced, was awarded custody of my sons, and spent the last twenty years raising them and running my business, hoping against hope to run into you, the woman I was and still am deeply in love with, or someone I would love just as much. But I know that wasn't going to happen because there's only one of you. So you see, Gail, you were not the home wrecker you thought you were. My marriage was on the rocks before we met! Our affair, in which I myself admitted to my wife, just pushed it to its inevitable end."

We caught up on a few other things, such as where we had been and what we had been doing, and talked a little about what might and hopefully be in our future. "In *our* future" sounded and felt so good, although I knew it would be a big mistake to think or even plan too far ahead. There was so much I could think of us doing together. Little did I know that the outcome of our first affair together would have a profound effect on our second chance to be together, the preordained curse of star-crossed lovers. Like the story of Romeo and Juliet, family would get in the way! Not mine this time; my sons would not stand in the way of my happiness nor I stand in the way of theirs.

Gail and I began spending as much time together as we could and, for the most part, having some good times. God, how I loved this woman! Gail was working for a company in a suburb north of the capital city. She began having problems concentrating on her job and wouldn't tell me the absolute reason why this was happening.

All she would tell me was that she was thinking about us so much, she couldn't do her job, and her employer was beginning to take notice. There was something more troubling her, but she wasn't ready to divulge it to me as of yet. I resigned myself not to push her for the answers and just let this take its natural course. Gail decided to take a two-week sabbatical from work to a spa in a state somewhat faraway for some R and R. Our second-chance relationship was now at the end of its third month, about the time our first one ended.

Against All Odds

On her return from the spa, she called me to say we needed to get together and talk about our future. Although my heart was full and overflowing, with love for her, I had a real bad feeling about this. She asked me to come by her place on Saturday afternoon because she had come to some conclusions and that was all she would tell me over the phone. The rest would and had to be face-to-face! On the ride to her place, I tried desperately not to come to any of my own premeditated conclusions. I forced myself to have an open mind and that I would have to accept whatever was coming next.

Besides, maybe this talk would be of good things for us; but whatever was about to be said and to happen, because I loved her as much as I did, good or bad news, I would have to face it with all the strength I could muster.

I was a little nervous when I got to her building's lobby and rang her to be buzzed in, thinking, *This just might be the last time I do this.* I really needed to stop being so gloomy and put a smile on my face. Didn't want her to see me looking so down. I made my way to her door, knocked, and heard her say from inside the door.

"Just a second, I'm coming!"

The door swung open; she stood looking down and not at me. I already knew what was coming next.

"Come in, Jim. Have a seat."

She didn't call me baby. In a heartbeat, this just went from bad to worse. She slowly approached me, stopped about six feet away. With her eyes looking at the floor between us, she began speaking softly, telling me why she wanted to see and talk to me today.

"Jim, I'm guessing you know what happened twenty years ago when I went home for a while after our breakup and attempted something stupid?"

"Yea, I heard about it, and I'm very glad you failed," I acknowledged.

"Okay, then you should have no trouble understanding that my family will not accept you in my life because they blame you and will not forgive and forget," she firmly stated, still not looking at me.

"This is not going to be easy on either of us, but we can't continue seeing each other. My family will never accept you in my life," she sadly proclaimed.

"You mean to tell me, after all this time, they can't forgive me?

You did, so why can't they?" I inquired.

"Because, Jim baby, they don't love you the way I do! I'm sorry. We can't go on seeing each other, as of today."

Ironic, isn't it? Twenty years earlier, I left her because of my family; and now twenty years later, she's leaving me because of her family! I guess we'd now come full circle.

Her eyes came up for a second; they appeared to be glazed over.

I stood up, took a deep breath. Knowing there wasn't anything I could do or say that would change things, I said, heavyhearted,

"Gail, because I truly love you, I must grant your request. But you must know I do this with a broken heart. Will you permit me a kiss good-bye?"

"Of course, I will. Come here," she answered and requested.

I slowly walked to her as she walked toward the door, savoring every second I had left to be with her. At the door, we embraced and kissed deeply for the last time. I heard her sigh very softly.

"Oh, Jim, baby."

We slowly let go of each other. I turned and opened the door and went into the hallway, turned to her, and said sadly, "I will miss you, Gail, and I will always feel love for you!" hoping against the odds she would recant what she said and tell me to stay. As she closed the door, all she said was, "Good-bye, Jim, and take good care of yourself, and please stop smoking!"

I slowly walked away, looking back a few times until her door was out of my line of sight, went down the elevator, and left the building.

Got in my little pickup truck, took a deep breath, and headed home. This hurt almost as much as losing my mother, but not so deep a loss that is as final as losing someone to death. Well, even though I had lost Gail once again, I did get my chance to sew up the loose ends of the events from twenty years ago; and that made my heart and head finally clear! As I said back then, there will always be a special place in my heart for Gail, here and now and perhaps in the afterlife! Maybe that's what we can take with us—our spent emotions, if nothing else!

Chapter Ten-Part Two

Reunions/Deceleration

August 1998

Where Is He?

I NOW FELT I needed to be among people in whom I had a mutual friendship with; the first place I could think of was the Castle Club's singles parties. I had been away from these for a while. And there wasn't anyone I knew from there that I stayed in contact with, outside of seeing them when I'd go there.

Now wondered if anything had changed, because things could change very fast around here, sometimes even virtually overnight!

I needed to go back and see if there were any significant changes.

It would be interesting to see how things were. I knew there would be people I wanted to see and there probably would be some people that I didn't want to see, but that's the risk I take!

On the other hand, having been in contact with Cheryl from time to time, I had a strong feeling that getting back with her wouldn't take much effort; what it would take was the desire to go back, and I didn't have that right now.

I've always believed that if something was or is meant to be, one way or another, it would or will be!

So if Cheryl and I should get back together, then somehow it would happen. When the next Thursday-night singles party came around, I found myself going there. At first, it seemed like all my old friends were there. As I walked around, mingling, I ran into most of the people I knew; but I didn't see Victor. Odd that he wouldn't be here, and then I thought for a minute, maybe he hadn't arrived yet or he was in the men's room. What I needed to do was ask someone who might know him, although I was a little afraid of what the answer might be. Victor was not a young man and there were some things I never bothered to find out about him. I just figured that what he wanted me to know about him, he would tell me. Out of respect, I didn't meddle into his life.

I spotted a woman I had seen Victor hang out with and dance with from time to time. I had been introduced to her by Victor before, but didn't have a lot of contact with her after that, so I approached her and said, "Hi, I'm Jim. I don't know if you remember me. We met the first night I met Victor, and I'm wondering where is he tonight because I don't see him here."

"Yes, I remember you, Jim. Victor isn't here tonight because he hasn't been feeling well and his doctor told him to get some rest so he's not coming out as much anymore for a while," she informed me.

I then realized I had never found out in what city he lived in, so I asked her if she knew. She told me, and to my surprise, all this time he was living right in my own city!

She would not give me his address because she told me that I needed to respect his privacy. Liking and respecting him as much as I did, I would not attempt to invade his private world.

I thanked her and went to the bar to get myself a drink, and to my pleasant surprise, I ended up standing next to my good ol' clubbing buddy Joe. He was just as surprised to see me as I was to see him. I never told him about these parties, figuring he wouldn't be interested in coming to them. We hung out for the evening and caught up on what we each had been doing. The night was an uneventful one, and I told Joe we needed to come back another night so he could meet Victor! He agreed that he would try.

No Beef Wellington!

Cheryl, knowing my birthday was getting very close, called me to invite me out for dinner to celebrate it with her. She explained that she would like to come up to my place and take me to a very nice restaurant in the capital city, using the reason that my city was closer to town than hers was. I could see the logic, but not what else she had in mind. She knew me well enough to accomplish a very successful seduction of me. And maybe I was ready for a retry with her; I had now seen painfully with Gail how important family could be to a woman, which helped me understand a little clearer the way Cheryl felt about hers.

She arrived at my house about seven thirty, and I was dressed and ready. The front doorbell rang, and I answered it, knowing it was Cheryl. My bedroom was just inside the front door through an archway to the right. She entered the bedroom and put her overnight bag on the bed, opened it, took out a black sheer baby-doll nightie out, and laid it spread out on the bed then looked at me and smiled.

I inquired innocently, "What this?"

"For later, if you're a good birthday boy!" she suggestively stated.

"Okay, Jim, you look ready. I'll drive. Come on, let's go!"

Off we went into the capital city to a very fancy restaurant. She had seen on the Web that they served beef Wellington, one of my favorite dishes. But to her disappointment, it wasn't on the menu for this particular night. No big deal, I would find something else to order.

Cheryl had problems with trying to please or make me happy because, for some reason or another, she usually fell short; but I have to give her an A for effort! I really felt that she just tried too hard; hell, once a woman knew what I liked, it would be a relatively simple task to accomplish. I just don't know why most of them didn't get it. This would happen more times than I care to remember. I really wasn't keeping count, just taking notice.

All in all, it was a very nice birthday dinner and night that began another chapter in the saga of Cheryl and Jim; we had now been in and out of each other lives for about three years, and we were going to try one more time.

I was now thinking that after what had happened with Gail—that for the past twenty years I was waiting for her and that second chance, and now that it has played itself out and we were not going to be together after all—I now felt, knowing this in my heart, I could openly commit to a relationship with no more chances and/or thoughts of Gail being in the wings. It was now time to move on emotionally.

Cheryl was the most likely candidate for me. After all, we did have some depth of feelings for each other and a history between us.

All Aboard!

Her birthday was now approaching, and I really wanted for it to be a very memorable one. I came up with something I had done before with Deenie, which was to stay over in that southeastern vacation place and partake in what was a very romantic three-hour dinner train ride on a vintage train in which you got the feeling you had traveled back in time to the forties! Cheryl and I popping in and out of each other's lives seemed like one or both of us were time-traveling through each other's lives! Anyway, my idea and plan to celebrate her thirty-ninth birthday could not have gone any better really!

(◊"Lost in a Minute"◊ Richard Elliot)

Welcoming 1999!

Nineteen ninety-nine was just over the horizon, and I wanted Cheryl and I to do something special and different to ring it in!

I figured we could plan this together, so we agreed to go to the hotel we had been patronizing in the southwestern vacation area because they had a New Year's Eve package, which was a room for two, dinner, and a New Year's Eve party in the basement lounge with the all the complementary accoutrements! The best part was that if you got a little drunk, you could just walk to your room and fall into bed, no driving! The price on this was extremely reasonable, so we made our reservations, and it turned out to be an excellent choice because we had a really good time.

I was, for the first time, feeling very confident about my feelings for Cheryl; and I wanted her to know this, so I did something I had not done before!

A Diamond in the Rough!

On a cold winter's night, I called Cheryl at her work and asked her to come by my house before she went home, because I had something for her and something to ask her! She had no clue what I was up to. I did it this way because if I had taken her out for a night of dining at a fancy restaurant for no apparent occasion, she would know something was up. I wanted her to be completely caught off guard when I presented her with a two-and-a-half-carat diamond engagement ring and a proposal of marriage! But before I would do this, I would give to her a large stuffed teddy bear. Up till then, I had only given her small ones to accompany any gifts I presented to her for celebrated occasions such as birthdays and the gift-giving holidays.

Well, I gave her the surprise of her life, and she accepted my proposal. So now we were engaged. She was the envy of all who saw her ring, and she seemed to be very proud of it, and truly happy. Our engagement looked like it was going to hold. We went along with no problems in our relationship for most of the year, discussing and planning on how we would we would proclaim our vows. We had several ideas, and we had to decide on one. We did agree to do it in the spring of 2001 or 2002, incidentally the year I turned fifty!

2000 Late Summer

Hook, Line, And Stinker

The year of two thousand proved to be to busy to get married because, my father had met an Asian woman half his age, that had him convinced that she was in love with him and my father fell for it, "Hook, Line, and Stinker" and agreed to marry her and the two of them would than move south. Which meant he wanted to sell the house where my oldest son Jim and I, lived on the first floor, sense nineteen seventy, the year my son was born. My younger sister was on the third floor and my dad was on the second. My son wanted to buy the house and asked his grandfather for the opportunity to do so. My father agreed, if he could come up with the money for it very soon, his price was the market value, less a small amount because the buyer is his grandson. Unfortunately, my son could not get the loan on his own so I would have to co-sign the loan and we would be fifthly, fifthly partners in the ownership of the house!

A Fool and His Money

My father told us that he needed the money for the house as soon as possible or he would sell it to someone else because he wanted to leave the state. So my son and I had to take the first approved loan we could get, and it wasn't a really good one because my father was in big hurry. Meantime, my sister moved out of the third floor so I could get it rented right away, and I did. We passed papers August 30, 2000, which meant it only took us four weeks to get the loan. He had his money, and when I inquired to when he would be leaving, he now told me he couldn't leave until November. I couldn't wait that long to get the apartment cleaned up and rented, he would have to pay me the rent for September and October. He didn't like that, but that's the way it had to be, or he wouldn't have to leave right away! He and his second wife left at the end of October, and I got the place rented in December. My son and I were real happy they were gone! Unsurprisingly, my father did not find what he had with his first wife; and so after about three years with his second wife, he was talking about a divorce, which I had heard in the grapevine!

All this business put a transitory hold on Cheryl and me getting married, and some other things were coming that would cause more delays, like Cheryl's bother being asked to leave his marital home because his wife was no longer happy with him and he came to live at Cheryl's house. The pressure was beginning to build, with three adults on the weekends and a teenager in a five-room house.

Cheryl's sister and cousin were now putting additions on their houses. And guess what? Cheryl now was talking about doing it to her house. Without getting into too many details, this would be the straw that broke the camel's back for our relationship. Her house addition project now took precedence over anything else, so our supposed engagement would suffer! With my announcement of leaving, Cheryl took off the ring, slammed it on the table. I took it and my things and left! As I walked out, thinking this would be the end of our relationship finally, any feelings we had between us were dying a long slow death. I really felt like this should be the last breakup for Cheryl and me. I was now very tired of our on-and-off, in-and-out relationship.

2004 Autumn

Everything Must Change

I had sent Cheryl an e-mail to inquire about her life, house, and well-being. This and a few telephone conversations to share news were the only way Cheryl and I had contact.

Cheryl had gotten deep under my skin, and it would take something devastating to get her out and put an end to our labored emotional association!

Something like a horrendous showing of the lack of love from one of us to the other. I had no clue what it could be at this time. I just knew it would take something that big to finalize whatever it was between Cheryl and me!

Some of the news I had was that in April, my father had died of a brain aneurysm. I felt no grief by this at all. I saw it as poetic justice. For DeeDee, if you remember, whom he had terrorized with forced sexual intent, had also suffered one of this but had survived it. The other more recent news was that after a little more than thirty years, I had decided to liquidate my independent distributorship food service business! It had gotten to the point where it was no longer lucrative enough to keep it going.

Cheryl's house project had been finished for a while now, and she and her daughter were enjoying all the extra room they had.

I told her my last official day of work would be October 30, 2004, and had no aspects of employment for myself and was not eligible to collect unemployment money. So I would have to find a job as soon as I could. She said she'd like to help me with this situation, which was nice to hear, for I had always helped her on things in any way I could. Once again, she would get an A for effort, but the job she helped me get had to be the worst job I had ever had! It was an overnight loss prevention wholesale house job with low-pay and horrible people to work with, and no real personal life because of sleeping days and working overnights. I lasted there nine weeks and then left abruptly. I started diligently looking for work using any and all avenues at my disposal.

2004 Early Winter

I'd had several job interviews and was on my way to one when I stopped to eat a fast-food lunch in my pick-up truck. Was almost finished with my lunch when my cell phone rang. It was a job offer from an interview I had three days earlier. A really good job with a decent salary, and I would be an employee of the company but be working out of my house. I accepted the job and would be sent an e-mail confirmation with orientation and training instructions. I then called and canceled the interview I was headed for. I was ecstatic with happiness; this would be my first job working for a company and getting benefits in thirty years! I had to tell someone; the first person I could think of calling was Cheryl to share this good news with. She was, to my surprise, glad for me and happy to hear from me; so I asked her to accompany me to a dinner celebration of my good fortune and a major change in my life!

After three days of orientation and training instructions, I started this new job of being the Energy Elite field representative in charge of servicing retailers that sold products that qualified for this program in a twenty-five-mile area of all the cities and towns north of my town. Because of the outstanding performance of my duties, it would be changed to a twenty-mile radius of the cities and towns around my town, which now included the capital city. This gave me the largest and most important area of all the seven Energy Elite field reps in my state; it felt like I was doing the work of two people, and it was realized later that I was! I really did like this new job very much and the people I started out working under and with. I didn't see much of Cheryl after the dinner celebration we had.

April 2005

Her Teeth! My Teeth!

After about four months or so into this new life of mine, I received a pleasantly surprising phone call from Deenie; it really was good to hear from her because, from time to time, I wondered how she was doing and now had the opportunity to find out. She informed me that she had been busy having major dental work done at the local dental school. I told her of my good fortune and that I now had dental insurance and I could use some work done too. For you see, my teeth were in bad shape; oh, they looked okay, but were very loose and gave me a lot of discomfort, and it now seemed like a good time to get something done about it.

I spent the next year or so having major dental work done; and Deenie—like an angel, God bless her—helped me through the two teeth extraction procedures I needed to have done. All my teeth needed to be removed, and I would be getting dentures; this wasn't as hard as it sounds because all my teeth were so loose they practically fell out on their own. The discomfort came in the healing of my gums. I took very little time off from my work for this. Being in the one-man operation profession, I have learned to work through the pain, like for instance running my one-man business for a time with a broken hand in a cast, aided only by what help my son Vincent could give me, God bless him! The work on my teeth took the better of two years before I was fully recovered; the upside to all this was, of course, I was no longer in any pain and discomfort because of my teeth and now had an awesome smile.

Late 2006

Deenie just seemed to disappear from my life. I surmised she had her own agenda that I didn't fit into. Considering all the help she had given to me, who was I to question her wanderlust? In any case, our latest relationship was only a good friendship with no benefits, as she would put it!

The Definitive Last Labor of Love

Feeling really good about my life now; the best I had felt in a long time. It had been so long, I couldn't remember ever feeling physically, mentally, and emotionally this good! I wanted to show off how good my life had become, and Cheryl was the first person I desired to see this.

(◊"Heavy Dose"◊ Count Basic)

With her birthday coming up, I requested she permit me to take her away for a four-day celebration of it to a waterfront town that we had been to before in the state southwest of us and enjoy ourselves. Without too much resistance, she agreed. So I made the arrangement, and we had a very good time for four days celebrating her birthday! We had come to an agreement to see each other, but nowhere as much or intense as in our past interactions. That was okay with me because maybe it was the intensity of the past times together that made them not work for too long, and this would be a totally new approach!

A Premature Bucket List?

2007

I don't know what it was but I felt as if I needed to get somethings done, somethings that I had been wanting do get done for some time now. I just looked at it as another effect of the accelerated life I had been living. I really wasn't that concerned with the reasons for this, and maybe I should have been. The holidays came and went with little interaction between Cheryl and me, although we did exchange gifts at Christmas, but only one or two each, and go out for a small holiday dinner. At this dinner, I told Cheryl of my desire to fulfill a few things in my life, and I'd like her to be there with me.

She asked me, "Jim, what are these things that you feel you now need to do?"

"Well, Cheryl, they're not really big things, and you may even think they're insignificant, but you could just humor me and come along for the pure fun of it!" I answered her and then told her what they were.

"Okay, there's really only two I'd like to start with, and these are to take a horse-drawn and open-sleigh ride in the snow and drive through an old wooden covered bridge."

"Jim, they sound fun and doable, so you make the arrangement and I will go with you!" she agreed.

Early March

These would have to happen in a time and place where both of the elements in my wish list would be available. I did the research and made all the arrangements for this to happen in one weekend getaway at the beginning of March in the year 2007. Cheryl was agreeable to this.

We left on a Friday afternoon in the first week of March, stayed at a very quaint northern inn where we were very close to the two events we had set out to do, which to our pleasure we did, as well as a few other activities we found while we were there! All in all, it was a good time for both of us!

On the way back home, Cheryl reminded me that she would be leaving soon to visit her sister in London, England, for ten days.

I had mentioned an interest in going with her; she wasn't agreeable to this and told me, "Maybe next time." I was okay with this because if she really wanted me to go with her, she would have asked me to; and she hadn't, so I dropped it and wished her a safe trip! And I'd see her when she got back. She had given me her sisters' home phone number, and I arranged with my cell phone provider for me to make calls to London without any high fees or problems.

In the first few days Cheryl was gone, just by chance, I happened to run into someone who knew Victor from the singles parties. I had not been to the parties or to the waterfront for quite a while, so I had been out of touch and was wondering about him. Sadly, they informed me that he had had a fatal heart attack and was gone to that big singles party in the sky. I will always be grateful for having met and known him!

R.I.P. good friend!

A Clandestine Embrace

March 19, 2007

   Life can throw at you something you may at first believe to be a cruel joke, but it can actually turn out be an event to educe an extreme change into your life and the way you see and think about it!
   Just such an event happened to me on a Monday morning, while I was leaving the house to go start my workday, feeling good and looking forward to doing some more of the things I hadn't gotten around to doing in my life yet! Dressed and ready to start my workweek, my briefcase in hand, I walked out my kitchen door into the back hall and, out of the blue, lost my balance and fell hard onto the floor on my left side. As I lay there, I realized that I couldn't move my left leg or arm and hand, and my cell phone was underneath me so I couldn't get to it. I tried to get up, but couldn't! My first thoughts were that my polio had come back and I would be living in that wheelchair that I had narrowly escaped as a child! Needless to say, I was very anxious of what might be happening to me and why.
   As I lay there, I could feel my right hand touching my left hand but couldn't move it. I thought to myself this paralysis has started on the left side and would most likely continue to affect the rest of me in time! At that moment, I heard what I figured was Pam, my second-floor tenant, walking in her kitchen above me. Thinking I could black out at any time, I called up to her; and thank God she heard me, opened her door, and asked me what I wanted.
   Not wanting to say, "I've fallen and can't get up," I simply said,
   "Pam, I'm on the floor, and I can't get myself up. Please call 9-1-1!"
   Pam then grabbed her cordless house phone and came down the stairs to see me on the floor, dialed 9-1-1, gave them the address, and informed them that I needed medical attention. She put her hand on my right shoulder and soothingly said, "Take it easy, Jim. They'll be here soon!"
   We both heard the siren coming closer; and very quickly, they picked me up, got me into the ambulance, and gave me a fast ride to the general hospital in the capital city five miles south; my attendant informed me that I was suffering a stroke! Everything was happening so fast, it seemed like a blur of events.

The next thing I remember was being put in the MRI machine, and about halfway in, they suddenly stopped. A doctor leaned into me and told me because the stroke had just happened within the last three hours, they had a drug that they called the Clog Buster that could cure me or kill me!

Feeling at that moment I had nothing to lose, I agreed to let them administer it! The first thing I felt was a warming sensation inside me, the next was a pins and needles sensation, and almost instantly, I could move my left hand and arm. I was also able to lift my left leg!

I was then transported to the intensive care unit, where I was adorned with two IVs, one was a blood thinner, and other things to monitor my condition. I finally got to talk to a doctor to ask what had happened to me and why. I was told that I had a clogged corroded artery on the right side of my neck just behind my ear. A piece of it broke off and went up into my brain. This clog had been forming for about the last twenty years because of my forty-year cigarette-smoking habit!

Who knew that smoking shrunk your arteries? I had never heard about that! I had my last cigarette the night before my stroke. During all this, my sons were contacted, and they came to the hospital to see me.

Cheryl was away in London, England, and was due back on the twenty-ninth. On my third day in the hospital, the doctors were contemplating a surgical operation to remove the clog on the morning of the fourth day in the hospital. I was told that if they decided to do this, I would only have a 30 percent chance of survival. I was okay with that because I figured if they didn't clear the clog, it would cause my death!

They had assigned me a recovery nurse named Gail, and I was asked if I'd like to see a priest; I refused the priest. Thinking this could be my last night in this life, I called Cheryl to hear her voice for possibly one last time and say good-bye in case I didn't make it; she wished me luck! She had now shown her true colors and her shallow depth of feelings for me. I then asked for a sleep aid and fell to sleep soon after taking it.

The morning came, and after one more ultrasound, I was informed that the doctors had decided not to operate because the risk factor was too high and there was no way they could lower it; they told me that if I kept my blood thin with medications, I should have no problems. I couldn't help but think that if this situation was reversed and it was Cheryl in the hospital and me away, I would have come home right away.

I was released from the hospital after a ten-day stay. At home, I would have to take some very potent blood-thinning medication to start with, two injections of Lovenox daily. I had made arrangements with Pam to do this for me and a visiting nurse to monitor my blood thickness once a week. As soon as it leveled off, I could start taking Coumadin tablets daily; and as time went on, I would eventually be on Plavix tablets for the rest of my life.

I tried to overlook the way Cheryl had reacted to my health problem and told her that I wasn't the same man anymore. There was no physical paralysis, but I did have some brain cell damage, and it would take quite a while for them to rebuild. And also, after being home for six weeks, I tried to go back to work in a part-time capacity, which only last about four months; it became too much for me to handle. Cheryl and I spent a little more time together, but the truth kept coming to the surface, and eventually, we couldn't stay together because of it. We had our final breakup the night before my fifty-sixth birthday on September 23, 2007.

After testing, I was awarded social security disability. I could now sit back and evaluate what to do with what was left of my life. I did feel a great sense of deceleration; the stroke had brought to a halt the accelerated way I had been living for so long! I always had a strong feeling that if I couldn't or didn't find a way to decelerate my life, then something would find me!

The first and hopefully not the last good thing to come out of having my stroke! So take this with you: good things can come from and out of bad things. There truly is a silver lining to that dark cloud!

Fini

Reflection

God Rest Her Saintly Soul!

All the women that came in and out of my life, I did have a measure of feelings for some more than others. They all gave me something to take with me on my journey through my life—either a lesson learned, memories, or both. I am truly grateful to them all. They all have a place in my heart and mind; a few have a place in my soul! As much as I desired for one of them to be Ms. Right, I didn't find her among them. Don't be saddened for me, for I have known love and been loved! But the only love I am sure was unconditional and real was the love my mother gave to me and I to her, and still do. God rest her saintly soul!

Mothers are the very special and the most important people in our world, for without them, we would not be here!

I truly wish you and yours good health and much happiness!

J. M. Valente

CPSIA information can be obtained at www.ICGtesting.com
Printed in the USA
267528BV00002B/38/P